Everyday Life: REFORM IN AMERICA

WALTER A. HAZEN

Good Year Books

An Imprint of Pearson Learning

Photo Credits

Front and back cover: *crowd border.* AP/Wide World Photos; *document background.* From the archives of the Seneca Falls Historical Society. Front cover: *t.l.* Jon Hammer/Archive Photos; *t.r.; b.* Corbis/Bettmann. 2: Smithsonian Institution. 3: The Metropolitan Museum of Art. 4: Library of Congress. 5: Sophia Smith Collection, Smith College. 10, 11: Library of Congress. 12: AP/Wide World Photos. 13: National Archives Trust Fund. 18: The Bettmann Archive. 19: Hulton Getty/Liaison Agency. 20: Corbis/Bettmann. 21: Oberlin College Archives. 26: U.S. Army Military History Institute. 27: National Library of Medicine. 28: Library of Congress. 29: The Granger Collection. 34: Hulton Getty/Liaison Agency. 35: Brown Brothers. 36: Culver Pictures. 37: Corbis/Bettmann. 42: Culver Pictures. 43: Lewis W. Hine/International Museum of Photography. 44: Culver Pictures. 45: Grant Smith/Corbis. 50: Library of Congress. 51: National Archives Trust Fund. 52: University of Illinois at Chicago, The Library, Jane Addams Memorial Collection. 53: UPI/Corbis/Bettmann. 54: Museum of the City of New York/ Archive Photos. 58: Archive Photos. 59: UPI/Corbis/Bettmann. 60: Corbis/Bettmann. 61: AFL-CIO. 66: Library of Congress. 67: Museum of the City of New York. 68, 69: Library of Congress. 74: S. Solom/ PhotoDisc, Inc. 75: Library of Congress. 76: The Bancroft Library. 77: Corbis/ Bettmann. 82, 83: Brown Brothers. 84: UPI/Corbis/Bettmann. 85: Library of Congress. 90: Corbis/Bettmann. 91: Library of Congress. 92, 93: UPI/Corbis/Bettmann.

Dedication

To Martha, Jordan, and Allison

Acknowledgments

Grateful acknowledgment to my editor, Laura Strom, who has guided me through several books in Good Year's "Everyday Life" series. Without her advice and support, this book would not have been possible.

I would also like to thank Roberta Dempsey, Acquisitions Manager at Good Year, for giving me the opportunity to be a part of such an exciting project. Her support and confidence in me is likewise appreciated.

 Good Year Books

are available for most basic curriculum subjects plus many enrichment areas. For more Good Year Books, contact your local bookseller or educational dealer. For a complete catalog with information about other Good Year Books, please write to:

Good Year Books
299 Jefferson Road
Parsippany, NJ 07054

Design and Illustration: Sean O'Neill, Ronan Design
Design Manager: M. Jane Heelan
Editor: Laura Layton Strom
Editorial Manager: Suzanne Beason
Executive Editor: Judith Adams

Table of Contents

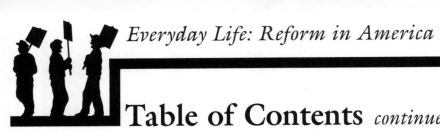

Table of Contents *continued*

Introduction

Immigrants preparing to leave for America in the 19th and early 20th centuries would have scoffed at the word *reform* mentioned in the same breath with the Land of Their Dreams. Reform? What was there to reform about America? America was the Garden of Eden! Its streets were paved with gold and its people went about in fancy carriages with money falling out of their pockets!

Or so the thinking went. As things turned out, America was crying out for reform. It was, to be sure, the most democratic nation in the world. But underneath the glitter were social, economic, and political ills that separated Americans into "Haves" and "Have Nots." The "Haves" enjoyed cushy jobs, comfortable homes, and political privileges. The "Have Nots," although not so severely persecuted as many had been in their native lands, were nonetheless relegated to the status of second-class citizens. And the millions of black people who either slaved or worked on these shores were in even worse straits.

What was so wrong with America in the 19th and 20th centuries that spurred dedicated reformers to action? The ills were many. Millions of blacks, as stated above, were subjected to the evils of slavery with little hope of freedom. Women could neither vote nor enter fields of work monopolized by men. Prisons and mental institutions were places of horror that often treated inmates like wild animals. Families and society were torn apart by alcohol abuse. Young children worked long hours in factories and mines. Adult workers labored for a pittance and had no way to address their grievances. Free blacks and immigrants lived in run-down slum areas with little chance to improve their lots.

In *Everyday Life: Reform in America*, you will learn how most of what was undemocratic and unfair about America has been slowly corrected. Much remains to be done, of course, but our country has come a long way in the last two centuries.

Walter A. Hazen

CHAPTER I

The Antislavery Movement

T he antislavery movement in America dates back to colonial times. In 1688, the Quakers of Germantown, Pennsylvania, were the first to publicly denounce the holding of slaves. Twelve years later, in 1700, a Massachusetts judge named Samuel Sewall wrote a paper condemning the existence of slavery in America. This was followed in 1775 by the founding in Philadelphia of the first antislavery society in the American colonies. The society was established by Benjamin Franklin and Dr. Benjamin Rush who gave it the unlikely name of the Society for the Relief of Free Negroes Unlawfully Held in Bondage. (Try saying that fast without swallowing your tongue!)

Thus, long before the word *abolitionist* (one who favored doing away with slavery) came into use in the early 1800s, there was a drive on to abolish the institution in the colonies. By the end of the 18th century, most of the Northern states had done just that. Rhode Island was the first in 1774. Vermont followed suit in 1777 and Pennsylvania in 1780. Then came Massachusetts in 1783, Connecticut and Rhode Island in 1784, and New York in 1799.

In 1787 Congress passed an ordinance (law) forbidding slavery in the Northwest Territory. This was a large region that extended from what is now Ohio to Wisconsin. The Ordinance of 1787 assured that slavery was doomed forever in the North.

Had it not been for the invention of the cotton gin in 1793 by Eli Whitney, slavery might also have gradually disappeared in the South. Virginia actually freed some 10,000 slaves in the years following the Revolutionary War, and other states were considering doing the same. But Whitney's gin made the growing of cotton profitable and called for an increase in the number of slaves to work on the cotton plantations. Strange as it may seem, an invention by a northerner helped strengthen slavery in the South.

Before the abolitionist movement began, there was an effort to return free blacks and freed slaves to Africa. Paul Cuffee, a free black man who had grown wealthy in the shipbuilding industry, was one of the first to propose such an idea. In 1812, he actually resettled

An early model of Eli Whitney's cotton gin. The cotton gin revolutionized cotton growing and strengthened the institution of slavery.

38 blacks in the British colony of Sierra Leone in West Africa. This number is really small when one considers that there were over 40,000 free blacks in America at the time.

Five years after Cuffee's endeavor, the American Colonization Society was founded. Its sole purpose was to encourage free blacks to resettle in Africa. John C. Calhoun of South Carolina and Henry Clay of Kentucky were among its organizers. They reasoned that black people would be interested in relocating to escape the prejudice and discrimination they faced in America. They even purchased a large tract of land in west Africa to that end. (This land later became the nation of Liberia.)

In response to the American Colonization Society's call for free blacks to resettle in Africa, a group of 3,000 prominent blacks met in Philadelphia in 1817. They were led by James Forten, a wealthy sailmaker who had fought in the Continental navy as a youth. Forten and others discouraged free blacks from accepting the American Colonization Society's offer. As a result, the Society's plans were not very successful. Only about 15,000 blacks emigrated to Africa between 1822 and the outbreak of the Civil War. Blacks refused to go for several reasons. Most, in spite of the prejudice and hardships they faced, considered America their home. Others had no desire to relocate to what they saw as the "wilds of Africa."

Free blacks and antislavery whites joined forces in the 1830s to launch the abolitionist movement. Prominent among white abolitionist leaders were Theodore Weld, Lucretia Mott, and William Lloyd Garrison. Theodore Weld was a Massachusetts reformer who dedicated his life to abolition. Lucretia Mott was a Quaker who fought for women's suffrage just as hard as she fought to end slavery. In 1833, she helped found the Female Antislavery Society in Philadelphia.

William Lloyd Garrison, one of the more extreme of the Northern abolitionists. His antislavery newspaper was often met with hostility in both the North and South.

William Lloyd Garrison was a Boston newspaper publisher who once burned a copy of the Constitution because it recognized slavery. In 1831, he started his own antislavery newspaper, *The Liberator*. In his weekly editions, Garrison called for an immediate end to slavery. He scoffed at the ideas of moderate abolitionists, who believed in gradual abolition and paying slaveowners for their losses. He even called for the North to secede from the Union. In 1833, he helped found the American Antislavery Society.

Black abolitionist Frederick Douglass, whose speeches and writings aroused Americans to the plight of slaves in the South.

The leading black abolitionist of the day was Frederick Douglass. Douglass was the son of a white Maryland slaveowner and a slave woman. As a youngster, he worked for a while as a house servant and was taught to read and write. In 1838, when he was 21, he escaped and went to Massachusetts. There he gained attention by making speeches against slavery. To avoid being captured and sent back to Maryland, he went to England for several years. He earned enough money lecturing in England and Ireland to return to the United States in 1847 and buy his freedom.

Douglass started his own antislavery newspaper, the *North Star*. He edited the paper until the outbreak of the Civil War, when he organized two regiments of black soldiers to fight for the North. Douglass was joined in his antislavery efforts by such prominent black abolitionists as Sojourner Truth and Harriet Tubman. Sojourner Truth, like Lucretia Mott, also became very active in the women's suffrage movement. Harriet Tubman was one of the main "conductors" on the Underground Railroad. Her heroics will be discussed later.

Abolitionists were supported by some of the leading writers of the day. Black writers Frances Harper and Joshua McCarter Simpson joined in the attack on slavery. So did such white authors as Ralph Waldo Emerson and John Greenleaf Whittier. Others of note were Henry David Thoreau, Walt Whitman, and James Russell Lowell. Thoreau even went to prison briefly for refusing to pay a tax he said went to support slavery.

To help escaped slaves flee to the North and to Canada, abolitionists organized the Underground Railroad. Don't be confused by the name; the Underground Railroad was no railroad at all, and it certainly was not underground. One story holds that the name came about when a group of slave catchers from Kentucky were chasing a runaway slave named Tice Davids. They followed Davids' trail to the Ohio River and watched him closely as he swam to the other side to freedom in Ohio. They saw him emerge from the river and then disappear completely. One of the slave catchers remarked that "he must have gone on an underground road."

The Underground Railroad was a series of routes and hideaways that enabled escaped slaves to reach freedom in the north. Levi Coffin, a white

Everyday Life: Reform in America, copyright © Good Year Books

Quaker, was the "president" of the railroad and directed its operations from Cincinnati. Both black and white abolitionists "worked" for the railroad, risking their lives daily to help slaves escape from a life of bondage.

The Underground Railroad had its own special terminology. Escaped fugitives were either passengers, freight, or merchandise. Guides who led them to freedom were conductors. Hiding places along the way were stations or depots. The person in charge of a station was the stationmaster. Escape itself was referred to as catching the next train.

Slaves being led along the Underground Railroad traveled at night. Often they were concealed in farm wagons under loads of produce. During the day, they hid in barns and homes that served as stations. Stationmasters provided them with food and other supplies they needed to continue their journey.

The most famous conductor on the Underground Railroad was Harriet Tubman. She was an escaped slave from Maryland who returned 19 times and guided more than 300 slaves along the road to freedom. On one trip she led her aged parents to safety in Auburn, New York. She and other "conductors" displayed great courage in light of the Fugitive Slave Law passed by Congress in 1850. This law required northerners to return escaped slaves to their owners and provided punishment for those who did not.

The Underground Railroad stayed in operation until the outbreak of the Civil War. During its short existence, it was responsible for about 75,000 slaves escaping to freedom. With the announcement of the Emancipation Proclamation abolishing slavery in 1863, "employees" of the railroad could look back with pride to their accomplishments.

Harriet Tubman (far left) with a group of freed slaves. Ms. Tubman risked her life to lead more than 300 slaves to freedom in the North.

As a postscript (addition) to the story of abolition, it should be pointed out that not every escaped slave chose to travel along the Underground Railroad. Others devised means of their own. Perhaps the most ingenious was Henry "Box" Brown of Richmond, Virginia. Brown had friends nail him inside a wooden box marked THIS SIDE UP and ship him to antislavery sympathizers in Philadelphia. How's that for creativity?

Name _____ Date _____

Name That Abolitionist

Many people were involved in the abolitionist movement. Thirteen of these are listed in the word box to the right. Select the correct name from the box and write it on the blank line in front of each statement.

Henry Brown	**Lucretia Mott**
John C. Calhoun	**Samuel Sewall**
Levi Coffin	**Henry David Thoreau**
Paul Cuffee	**Sojourner Truth**
Frederick Douglass	**Harriet Tubman**
Benjamin Franklin	**Eli Whitney**
William Lloyd Garrison	

1. _____ "I invented the cotton gin."

2. _____ "I was a conductor on the Underground Railroad."

3. _____ "I lectured in England and Ireland and saved enough money to buy my freedom."

4. _____ "I was known as 'Box' because of the way I escaped to Philadelphia."

5. _____ "I was a Massachusetts judge who condemned slavery as early as 1700."

6. _____ "I helped found the Female Antislavery Society."

7. _____ "I was imprisoned for refusing to pay a tax I thought supported slavery."

8. _____ "I was a black female abolitionist who was also active in the women's suffrage movement."

9. _____ "I was 'president' of the Underground Railroad."

10. _____ "I helped send 38 free blacks to Sierra Leone in 1812."

11. _____ "I helped found the American Colonization Society."

12. _____ "I published the antislavery newspaper *The Liberator*."

13. _____ "I helped establish the Society for the Relief of Free Negroes Unlawfully Held in Bondage."

Everyday Life: Reform in America, copyright © Good Year Books

Name _____ Date _____

Solve Some Antislavery Word Problems

Below are four word problems associated with the antislavery movement. Space is provided for you to work, along with lines on which to write your answers.

1. The Underground Railroad was in existence for about 30 years. During that time, some 75,000 runaway slaves traveled it to freedom. What was the average number of slaves who "rode" the railroad each year?

_____ slaves

2. At the time the Civil War began, there were approximately 4,000,000 black people in America. About 500,000 of these were free. What percent of the total black population was free?

_____ percent

3. About 97% of free blacks in America turned down the American Colonization Society's offer to transport them to Africa. This meant that _____ free blacks refused to be resettled.

4. It took Daniel, a runaway slave, a full year to make his way 730 miles to freedom across the Ohio River. How many miles did he average each day?

_____ miles

Name _____ Date _____

Keep an Underground Railroad Diary

Imagine you are a runaway slave traveling with a group along the Underground Railroad in 1851. Keep a two-day diary of events that might have taken place along the way.

July 10, 1851

Dear Diary,

_____

_____

_____

_____

_____

_____

_____

_____

_____

_____

_____

_____

_____

_____

_____

_____

_____

_____

_____

_____

_____

July 11, 1851

Dear Diary,

_____

_____

_____

_____

_____

_____

_____

_____

_____

_____

_____

_____

_____

_____

_____

_____

_____

_____

_____

_____

_____

Everyday Life: Reform in America, copyright © Good Year® Books

Name _____ Date _____

Use Your Critical-Thinking Skills

Using the lines provided, write your best answers to the questions.

1. Tell why you agree or disagree with the statement: "Free blacks would have been better off had they accepted the American Colonization Society's offer to resettle in Africa."

   _____

   _____

   _____

2. The Fugitive Slave Law of 1850 provided harsh fines and even imprisonment for anyone who aided a runaway slave. If you had lived in the North at the time, would you have agreed to hide fugitive slaves on your property? Why or why not?

   _____

   _____

   _____

3. Imagine yourself living at the time of the antislavery movement, and you have decided to take up the cause of abolition. Would you favor an immediate or gradual freeing of the slaves? Give reasons why you feel as you do.

   _____

   _____

   _____

4. Tell why you agree or disagree with the statement: "The Civil War was inevitable and would have occurred even if slavery had been abolished long before 1861."

   _____

   _____

   _____

Everyday Life: Reform in America, copyright © Good Year Books

CHAPTER 2

Women's Rights

For more than two centuries, women in America were expected to stay home and be content with being wives and mothers. They were not permitted to participate in politics or even to speak at meetings. After being allowed to work, they had to turn over their hard-earned wages to their husbands. Finally, in the event of divorce, they stood helplessly by as their husbands were awarded custody of the children.

The above conditions were the rule in America from colonial times to the 19th century. The Supreme Court, even as late as 1872, ruled that the role of women in society was to fulfill the responsibilities of wifely duties and motherhood. It was indeed a man's world. It was a world that women did not understand (according to men) and from which they were almost totally barred.

Lucretia Mott, one of the leaders of the women's rights movement. She helped organize the first women's rights convention in 1848.

Women might have remained second-class citizens even longer had it not been for an occurrence in 1840. In that year, the World Anti-Slavery Convention held its conference in London, England. A number of women accompanied their husbands to the event, two of these being Lucretia Mott and Elizabeth Cady Stanton from the United States. Mrs. Mott went as a representative of the American Female Antislavery Society. Mrs. Stanton was on her honeymoon and naturally accompanied her husband, who was a delegate. What happened when the convention opened infuriated both women and helped launch the women's rights movement in America.

Both Lucretia Mott and Elizabeth Cady Stanton looked forward to participating in the discussions that took place at the convention. But that was not to be. Not only were they denied participation but they were forced to sit in the galleries behind closed curtains! Can you imagine how angry and humiliated they were?

Lucretia Mott and Elizabeth Cady Stanton did not know each other before the antislavery convention. They met by accident while strolling the streets of London. Once acquainted, they began to share how they felt about being snubbed by the male delegates at the conference. The more they talked, the more they were determined to do something about it. They left England intent on holding a women's rights convention in the United States.

Everyday Life: Reform in America, copyright © Good Year Books

Eight years passed before the new friends realized their dream. Both were wives and mothers; home "duties" came first. Finally, in July 1848, the convention was held at Seneca Falls, New York. It was attended by more than 300 people, of whom some 30 were men. (One gentleman of note was the famous antislavery leader Frederick Douglass.) Participants came from as far as fifty miles away, traveling by every possible means. Some even walked. One young farm girl who rode a horse to the conference lived to see the day when women nationwide won the right to vote. Her name was Charlotte Woodward. She was 91 years old when the 19th Amendment became a part of the Constitution in 1920.

Elizabeth Cady Stanton, a contemporary of Lucretia Mott, who devoted her life to women's rights and other liberal causes.

Before the Seneca Falls convention began, five women, led by Elizabeth Cady Stanton and Lucretia Mott drew up a declaration. They called it the Declaration of Sentiments. In many ways, it resembled the Declaration of Independence. It began with a Preamble, or introduction. It then listed all the grievances women had against the male-dominated society in which they lived. In short, the Declaration demanded that women should have equal rights with regard to education, property, and employment.

No one in attendance objected to the above demands. But one grievance written into the Declaration by Elizabeth Cady Stanton caused an uproar. That was the demand for the right to vote. Few men in the United States were ready to grant such a privilege to women. Women had no business engaging in politics, they would say. Women did not understand such matters as government and were likely to vote foolishly, they would continue. More importantly, they would insist that woman's place was in the home, taking care of children and household chores.

The voting plank (part) of the Declaration was saved by Frederick Douglass. He maintained that it did not make sense to fight for the right of black men to vote without including black women. And if black women were included in the demand, then white women should also be included. With this argument, the convention passed the Declaration of Sentiments.

Shortly after the Seneca Falls convention, women began to organize on a national level. Soon the main issue of the movement became the *suffrage*, or

the right to vote. Elizabeth Cady Stanton and Lucretia Mott were joined in this effort by the likes of Susan B. Anthony and others.

In 1869, the women's rights movement split into two groups. One invited men to join and sought to win the vote at the state level. It was led by Lucy Stone and her husband, Henry Blackwell. The other denied men membership and petitioned Congress for a constitutional amendment granting women the suffrage. Prominent among the leaders of this second group were Elizabeth Cady Stanton and Susan B. Anthony.

The group that favored winning the suffrage battle at the state level enjoyed success first. In 1869, Wyoming became the first state to give women the vote. Utah followed in 1870, Colorado in 1893, and Idaho in 1896. Then, in 1912, Kansas, Arizona, and Oregon did the same.

In 1890, the warring factions (groups) of the women's movement united to form the National American Woman Suffrage Association. Its first president was Susan B. Anthony. Little changed, however. The new association was just as divided as the two groups that formed it had been. This time, it was split between moderates and militants. Moderates favored working within the law and getting things done through cooperation with legislators. Militants, on the other hand, had little patience with such methods. They proposed using such methods as demonstrations and marches to attain their goal.

The tactics used by women to gain the vote grew even more aggressive at the turn of the 20th century. Lucy Stone died in 1893, followed by Elizabeth Cady Stanton in 1902 and Susan B. Anthony in 1906. New leadership

Alice Paul (second from the right) and other suffragettes demonstrate at the 1920 Republican National Convention in Chicago. The 19th Amendment granting women the right to vote was ratified two months later.

appeared that carried the women's protest to a higher level. For the first time, *suffragettes*, as women who campaigned for the vote were called, began to speak on street corners and at the gates of factories. In January 1917, they began to picket the White House.

Suffragettes such as Alice Paul and Lucy Burns had participated in the women's suffrage movement in England. They had demonstrated alongside their British peers and gone to prison for their actions. They had been force-fed when they refused to eat and beaten and humiliated at every turn. They were ready and well-prepared to use the same tactics in America.

Everyday Life: Reform in America, copyright © Good Year Books

The summer of 1917 saw the women's suffrage movement come to a climax. Pickets kept the heat on the White House, causing no small amount of embarrassment to President Woodrow Wilson. Matters turned ugly. While police stood by and did nothing, some male bystanders vented their rage on the suffragettes. Alice Paul, Lucy Burns, and others were cursed, beaten, and kicked. Finally, they were arrested and thrown into prison. There they were subjected to the same inhumane treatment that suffragettes had faced in England. Alice Paul and Lucy Burns almost died from the treatment they received.

By the end of summer the American people had had enough. Some of the women imprisoned were elderly and frail. Others were the wives of government officials and prominent members of the Democratic Party. Faced with mounting pressure, the House of Representatives in January 1918, passed the 19th Amendment giving women the vote. The Senate did the same the following year. In August 1920, the amendment was ratified (approved) by the states and became a part of the Constitution. (African-American women, like African-American men, would have to wait another 45 years to realize the suffrage in some states.)

The fight for the suffrage was only the beginning of the women's rights movement. During World War II, women came out of the home and took jobs in factories and other places of employment. So many men had gone off to fight that the labor of women was needed. After the war, however, female workers were told to go home and take care of their household duties.

Little changed in the struggle for women's rights until 1963. In that year, Betty Friedan published a book entitled *The Feminine Mystique.* In her research, Ms. Friedan found that most American women were not completely satisfied with their roles as wives and homemakers. A large number wanted and expected more out of life, such as jobs and careers. Three years later, Ms. Friedan and 27 other women founded NOW, the National Organization for Women.

Thanks to the efforts of NOW and other groups, women have made great strides toward equality since the 1970s. In spite of their achievements, however, discrimination still exists against women in all areas. Until such discrimination ends, women can never feel that they enjoy full equality with their male counterparts.

Susan B. Anthony in later life. In addition to women's rights, she was also at the forefront in the temperance and antislavery movements.

Name _____ Date _____

Write an Article for the *Seneca Falls Journal*

Imagine you are a reporter for the *Seneca Falls* (New York) *Journal* at the time the women's convention assembled in that city. On the lines provided, write a short article that would go along with the headlines. Be sure to include answers to the five "W" questions: Who? What? When? Where? and Why?

The Seneca Falls Journal

★ ★ ★ ★ ★ ★ ★ ★ ★ ★ ★ ★ ★ ★ ★ ★ ★ ★ ★

***** July 12, 1848 *****

WOMEN'S CONVENTION OPENS TODAY
LARGE GATHERING EXPECTED

_____
_____
_____
_____
_____
_____
_____
_____
_____
_____
_____
_____
_____
_____
_____
_____
_____
_____
_____
_____

Name _____ Date _____

Solve a Women's Rights Crossword

ACROSS

3. She wrote *The Feminine Mystique.*

4. First name of suffragettes Stone and Burns.

6. Elizabeth Cady _____

9. _____ Douglass

12. Susan B. _____

14. First state to grant women the suffrage.

DOWN

1. Lucretia Mott and Elizabeth Cady Stanton met in this city.

2. President at the time of the 19th Amendment.

5. The right to vote.

7. _____ Paul

8. _____ Falls, New York.

10. _____ Mott

11. Second state to permit women to vote.

13. Initials of the National Organization for Women.

Name _____ Date _____

Write a Letter

Imagine you are living in the year 1917. Write a letter to your Congressman, Representative Thaddeus Talkalot, asking that he support the proposed constitutional amendment guaranteeing women the right to vote. Give reasons why you think the amendment should be passed.

August 14, 1917

The Honorable Thaddeus Talkalot,
House of Representatives,
Washington, D.C.

Sir:

_____

_____

_____

_____

_____

_____

_____

_____

_____

_____

_____

_____

_____

_____

_____

_____

_____

_____

Sincerely,

_____

Name _____ Date _____

Distinguish Between Fact and Opinion

Remembering that a fact is something that can be proven while an opinion is only a strong belief, decide which term fits each of the statements.

Write **F** if you think a sentence is a fact. Write **O** if you consider it only an opinion.

_____1. Men are more intelligent than women.

_____2. Women are more intelligent than men.

_____3. In today's society, there are men who willingly stay home and fulfill the role of homemaker while their wives work.

_____4. Most men handle stress better than their female counterparts.

_____5. Most men are physically stronger than women.

_____6. A woman will no doubt be elected president in the not-too-distant future.

_____7. Women have proven to be just as capable in politics as men.

_____8. If given a choice in a presidential election, most women would vote for a female candidate over a male opponent.

_____9. Alice Paul and Lucy Burns both favored radical methods in attaining the right to vote.

_____10. Madeleine Albright, Secretary of State in President Clinton's cabinet, is the most capable person to ever hold that position.

_____11. Women in colonial times enjoyed few civil rights.

_____12. Wyoming was the first state to grant women the right to vote.

_____13. Until Betty Friedan wrote *The Feminine Mystique*, most women were satisfied in their role as homemakers.

_____14. Abolitionist Frederick Douglass was a strong supporter of women's rights.

CHAPTER 3

Education

I magine that you broke a class rule or failed to turn in a homework assignment. As punishment, your teacher has determined that you must stay in after school one day for an hour. You are sore; you had big plans for that particular afternoon, and now those plans are in shambles. Besides, you know you will also "catch it" from your parent(s) or guardian when you get home. And then there's the additional possibility that you have a big brother or big sister to rub it in and make it even worse.

If the children of colonial New England could make an appearance today, you certainly would receive no sympathy from them. Stay after school for an hour, indeed! They would be quick to tell you that they would have welcomed such mild punishment. In colonial times, whippings and tongue-lashings were everyday occurrences, and often the discipline was much harsher. The cleft stick is a case in point. An unruly child was made to go outside and break a "switch" from a tree. The teacher then cut a cleft, or slit, in the broken end, pried it apart to the desired degree, and clamped it on the nose or tongue of the mischief-maker. Yes, it hurt! And it might be left on for hours!

Himself a teacher for many years, the author is aware that teachers today also have complaints. Sometimes this has to do with salary, and justly so. But consider the poor teachers of colonial times. Usually they received no pay at all; they lived by rooming and eating with the families of their students. But there is more. In addition to their instructional duties, teachers in New England were expected to perform certain tasks in the community. There were even times when they had to double as grave diggers at the local cemetery!

Education in colonial times was linked to religion. Church leaders believed everybody should be able to read the Bible, and to do so they had to learn to read. In 1642, the Massachusetts Bay Colony passed a law requiring that all children be instructed in reading. The Massachusetts General School Act followed in 1647. This law required that a town of at least 50 families had to hire an elementary school teacher. Towns of over

A girl reads aloud in a colonial school. In spite of harsh discipline, colonial students did not always pay attention to the lesson in progress. From the Bettman Archives.

Everyday Life: Reform in America, copyright © Good Year Books

100 families had to have a Latin grammar school. Other New England colonies passed similar laws, and public education in America was born.

Colonial elementary schools were called *dame schools*, the word *dame* as used here meaning schoolmistress, or teacher. Usually the teacher was an elderly widow who held classes in her home. While the children went about their lessons, the dame took care of her personal chores. The curriculum of a dame school consisted of reading, writing, arithmetic, and religion.

Most colonial children attended school for only three years. Adults thought that was all the education a person required, especially girls. After all, they reasoned, girls needed only to acquire those skills necessary to make them good wives and mothers. Some men even believed that too much education would cause insanity in young ladies! As for boys, those few who did not go on to a Latin grammar school were apprenticed to a craftsman to learn a trade.

Some New England towns funded common schools. Common schools provided students with several additional years of education. The typical common school consisted of a one-room schoolhouse heated with a fireplace. This kind of school remained prevalent in America through the years of the last frontier and, in some areas, well into modern times.

Harvard University in 1638, the year its name was changed from Cambridge College.

Large towns such as Boston had Latin grammar schools. Here promising boys were prepared for careers as ministers, lawyers, or doctors. They learned Latin and some Greek, and they usually graduated when they were about fifteen. Afterwards, they might move on to Cambridge College for advanced study. Cambridge College was founded in Cambridge, Massachusetts, in 1636. It was the first institution of higher learning in America. In 1638, Cambridge became known as Harvard.

In the Middle Colonies, each church ran its own schools. There were Quaker schools, Anglican schools, and Catholic schools. In the South, education was never a major priority. The sons of wealthy landowners were either taught by tutors or sent to England to be educated. Girls received only

Everyday Life: Reform in America, copyright © Good Year Books

Horace Mann, who pioneered the drive for public education in America.

enough education to make them good homemakers. The children of common people received no education at all.

Although the idea of public education began in the 17th century, the schools established in the colonies were not free. Some tax money went toward that purpose, but, in general, students paid their own way. Almost 200 years passed before free education on the elementary level became a reality.

A leader in the drive for free and better education was Horace Mann. Mann served in the Massachusetts state legislature for many years, where he was responsible for the founding of several teachers' colleges. These colleges, called "normal schools" at the time, offered a two-year course of study to prepare young people to teach.

In 1837, Mann left the state legislature to become the head of the Massachusetts Board of Education. Through his leadership, Massachusetts set a standard in education that was later adopted by other states. Better schoolhouses were built and well-trained, better-paid teachers hired to staff them. Students were divided into grades for the first time, and the school year was extended to six months. The curriculum was broadened to include a wider range of subjects, and improved textbooks came into use. Because of his efforts, Horace Mann is often referred to as the "Father of the Common School" or the "Father of Public Education."

By 1850, most of the northern states had established free elementary schools. Mann and others then began the fight for free public high schools. (One public high school had already opened in 1821 in Boston.) Schools were also founded to serve the needs of the blind, the deaf, and other handicapped students.

Public education was slow to develop in the South and on the frontier. As has already been mentioned, education in the South was confined to children of large plantation owners. Little would change there until after the Civil War. On the frontier, rugged pioneers viewed too much "book larnin" with a distrustful eye. In their opinion, the "three R's" — 'reading, 'riting, and 'rithmetic were all a youngster needed to make his or her way in the world.

Following Boston's example in 1821, other cities began to collect taxes to support public high schools. At first high schools were just for boys. Then

Everyday Life: Reform in America, copyright © Good Year Books

cities began to build such schools for girls. The first city to have a high school where boys and girls attended together was Chicago in 1856. In 1909, the first junior high school opened in Berkeley, California.

Early high schools did not concern themselves with preparing students for college. Gradually, however, high schools took on this function. In time, the needs of gifted students and students with special needs were also addressed. Today there are classes designed to meet the needs of students at every level and learning capability.

Another innovation in education that occurred in the United States in the mid-1800s was the kindergarten. *Kindergarten* is a German term that means "garden for children." Friedrich Froebel established the first kindergarten in Germany in 1837. Its purpose was to better prepare young children to begin their formal education in the first grade.

The first kindergarten in the United States was established in 1855 in Watertown, Wisconsin. It was a private school founded for the children of German immigrants. A kindergarten for English-speaking students was established in Boston, Massachusetts, in 1860. The first public kindergarten appeared in St. Louis, Missouri, in 1873.

Colleges were started in the United States long before high schools and kindergartens. After Harvard was founded in 1636, such prestigious colleges as Yale, Columbia, Rutgers, and Dartmouth were established. At first, women were denied the privilege of a college education, but this began to change in the early 1820s. The Troy Female Seminary in Troy, New York, opened in 1821, followed by Mt. Holyoke College in South Hadley, Massachusetts, in 1838. The first all-male school to admit women students was Oberlin College in Ohio in 1834. It was also the first college to admit African-Americans.

Oberlin College in Oberlin, Ohio. Founded in 1833 as an all-male school, it opened its doors to women the following year.

Reforms that have taken place since the early 1800s have made education available to all Americans. While it is true that public schools today face many problems (drugs and student violence to name two), there is no denying that a good education is within the reach of all students who apply themselves.

Name _____ Date _____

Compare Colonial Schools with Modern Schools

On the lines below the headings "Colonial Schools" and "Modern Schools," write pertinent facts about each.

	Colonial Schools	**Modern Schools**
1. Type of school building	_____	_____
	_____	_____
2. Heating	_____	_____
3. Subjects studied	_____	_____
	_____	_____
4. Teacher qualifications	_____	_____
	_____	_____
5. Discipline	_____	_____
	_____	_____
6. Length of school year	_____	_____
7. Number of years attended	_____	_____
8. Attitude toward education for girls	_____	_____
	_____	_____

Everyday Life: Reform in America, copyright © Good Year Books

Name _____ Date _____

Use Your Critical-Thinking Skills

Think about the questions concerning education that are presented. Then write your best answer to each on the lines provided. Continue on a separate sheet of paper if you need more space for some answers.

1. Why do you think all states have compulsory education laws that require children to attend school to a certain age?

   _____

   _____

   _____

2. How do you feel about parents home-schooling their children? Are there any benefits to such a practice? Any drawbacks? Would you personally want to be home-schooled? Why or why not?

   _____

   _____

   _____

3. Should all children be expected to go to college? Why or why not? Should all children be given the opportunity? Why or why not?

   _____

   _____

   _____

4. Many critics maintain that education in the United States is far inferior to that of such countries as Japan. Do you agree or disagree with this assertion? Why?

   _____

   _____

   _____

Name _____ Date _____

Test Your Knowledge of Massachusetts

How much do you know about Massachusetts, the state where education in America got its start?

The eleven questions on this page have to do with Massachusetts and its history. See how many you can answer correctly without referring to your textbook or some other source. Underline each correct answer from the three offered in parentheses.

1. Massachusetts is bordered on the east by the (state of Maine, Atlantic Ocean, state of Rhode Island).

2. Two states border Massachusetts to the north. They are (Vermont and New Hampshire, Maine and Rhode Island, Connecticut and New York).

3. West of Massachusetts is the state of (Pennsylvania, Connecticut, New York).

4. The capital of Massachusetts is (Springfield, Cambridge, Boston).

5. Boston, Massachusetts' largest city, is located in the (eastern, southern, western) part of the state.

6. A fish often associated with Massachusetts is the (cod, trout, catfish).

7. In 1620, the Pilgrims established a colony in Massachusetts at (Salem, Plymouth, Nantucket).

8. Squanto was (a village south of Boston, a kind of early squash grown in Massachusetts, an Indian who befriended and helped the Pilgrims).

9. Many well-known persons were born in Massachusetts. One was Clara Barton, who (founded the American Red Cross, made contributions to early education, was a leader in the women's suffrage movement).

10. Emily Dickinson was another famous Massachusetts native. She was a (teacher, poet, nurse).

11. Surely you have heard of Eli Whitney, yet another well-known person born in Massachusetts. Whitney gained fame as a(an) (writer, statesman, inventor).

Everyday Life: Reform in America, copyright © Good Year Books

Name _____ Date _____

Solve Some Schooling Math Problems

Listed in the box are seven colonial children and the number of years each attended school. Review mean, median, mode, and range in your mathematics book. Then answer the questions pertaining to the chart.

Student	Number of Years Attended School
Sarah	3
Jonathan	7
Miles	9
Naomi	3
Aaron	8
Ruth	2
Jeremiah	10

1. What is the total number of years attended by the seven students? _____ years

2. What is the mean? _____ years

3. Is there a mode? If so, what is it? _____

4. What number represents the median? _____

5. What is the range? _____

6. How many more years did Miles and Jeremiah attend school than Sarah and Ruth? _____ years

7. How many more years did the boys attend school than the girls? _____ years

8. When you graduate from high school, you will have received _____ more years of education than Ruth and _____ more years than Jonathan.

CHAPTER 4

Prisons and Asylums

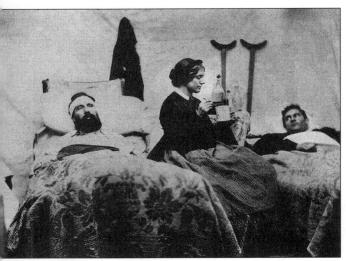

A nurse dispenses medicine in a hospital during the Civil War. Nurses at that time were held to the highest of moral standards.

D orothea Lynde Dix was a woman not be trifled with. A teacher at the tender age of 14 and founder of her own school for girls at 19, she was quick to apply the whip where it hurt the most to any young lady who incurred her wrath. Years later, as Superintendent of Nurses in the Civil War, she was equally as strict with her nurses. One of her cardinal rules was that "all nurses are required to be plain-looking." Ms. Dix had little patience with young girls who were more interested in finding husbands than in tending the sick and wounded. In addition, all applicants had to be above the age of 30 and could wear no jewelry. I think you might agree that Dorothea Dix was a rather tough "drill sergeant!"

In the first three chapters of this book, you learned that there were a number of reformers who led the way in getting slavery abolished, winning the suffrage for women, and improving the educational standards of schools. But when it came to reforming the deplorable conditions in America's asylums and prisons, it was, for the most part, a one-person show. And that person was Dorothea Lynde Dix.

Dorothea Dix became a reformer quite by accident. One Sunday in March 1841, she filled in for a Sunday-school teacher at the East Cambridge House of Corrections in Massachusetts. She was shocked by what she found. Her class consisted not only of hardened criminals but mentally ill persons as well. It was then that she realized it was the custom to keep people suffering from mental illness behind bars like dangerous beasts. Her discovery launched her into a career of reform that would continue until she was 80 years old.

After her experience that Sunday, Dorothea Dix visited every jail and poorhouse in Massachusetts over the next two years. What she found and observed was stunning. Insane inmates were kept chained in cages, closets, cellars, and stalls. Often they were naked. In the town of Medford, she found one man who had been confined in a small stall for 17 years. In Granville, she saw another who had been in a stall for so long that he had lost the use of his arms and legs due to the lack of exercise.

Everyday Life: Reform in America, copyright © Good Year Books

There is more. Ms. Dix noted that the places in which the mentally ill were kept were unheated in winter and stifling hot in summer. This was in keeping with the widely accepted belief at the time that the insane did not feel extremes of temperature. Therefore, they had no need for heat or cool air. If they complained of their lot, they were beaten into submission by their jailers wielding rods. What was even more heartbreaking is that Ms. Dix found that many of these poor souls were not insane at all. A large number were either feeble-minded, deaf, or blind.

Angry and moved by her experiences, Dorothea Dix in 1843 challenged the Massachusetts state legislature to fund asylums for the mentally ill. At the time, there were only eight such institutions in all of the United States. She pointed out in her *Memorial to the Legislature of Massachusetts* that the public was both ignorant of and indifferent to the plight of the insane and that government action was needed to save such persons from the horrible treatment they received in prison. The legislature was impressed by her presentation and listened intently as she described conditions throughout the state. Because of her report, the state of Massachusetts was one of the first to take action to help the mentally ill.

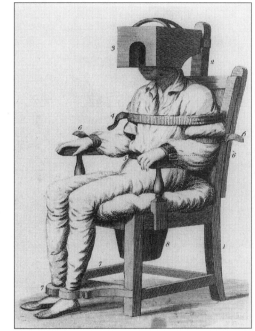

A "tranquilizing chair" thought to calm mental patients. Such impractical methods were common in early asylums.

Dorothea Dix carried her fight to aid the insane throughout the United States. What she found in other places mirrored conditions in Massachusetts. People guilty of nothing more than having mental or learning problems were routinely chained, beaten, and kept in cellars and stalls. Men, women, and children, whether sane or insane, were thrown together in the same jails and poorhouses. Ms. Dix traveled thousands of miles to expose the plight of these helpless people. As a result, 20 states soon followed Massachusetts' example and established asylums for the mentally ill.

In 1854, Dorothea Dix carried her reform movement to Europe. She had audiences with Queen Victoria in England and Pope Pius IX in Rome. She convinced both to take measures to improve the treatment of the insane. While across the Atlantic, she also worked for reform in France, Greece, and Russia. Special hospitals for the mentally ill were built in those countries because of her work. She even traveled to Japan and was instrumental in having the first asylum for persons with mental problems constructed there.

While Dorothea Dix was campaigning for better treatment for the mentally ill, she also petitioned state legislatures to do the same for criminals. Some mention has already been made of the terrible conditions in the nation's prisons. Prisoners were kept in dark and dirty cells. Children were placed together with hardened criminals. Food was poor and medical care almost nonexistent. Punishment was severe and often at the whim of cruel jailers. No thought was given to rehabilitating prisoners to cope with life after their release. In the eyes of the public, prison inmates were unworthy of any special consideration.

Dorothea Dix, a leading 19th century social reformer. Her humanitarian efforts resulted in better treatment for criminals and the mentally ill.

Ms. Dix and others also attacked and brought to an end the practice of imprisoning people for debt. Can you believe someone was once thrown into jail for a debt of six cents? It is true. One prison in America in the 1830s contained 24 inmates who had been jailed for owing from 6 to 90 cents! (One wonders what the sentence might have been for some unfortunate soul who owed a dollar!) If such a practice still existed today, the vast majority of Americans would probably spend some part of their lives behind bars.

As was true with the antislavery movement, one of the first groups in America to consider prison reform were the Quakers. They believed that inmates should not suffer physical punishment and that efforts should be made to rehabilitate or change them. Unfortunately, their method of rehabilitation created more problems than it cured. Beginning in 1790 in the Walnut Street Jail in Philadelphia, prisoners were placed in solitary cells, where it was believed that private meditation would change their attitudes and behavior. But the only result of isolating inmates to think about what they had done was that many suffered complete nervous and mental breakdowns. Consequently, the Quaker method had to be modified.

The Auburn New York Prison, built in 1819, adopted the Quaker method but changed it considerably. While prisoners were kept in separate cells, they ate together in the prison dining room and worked side by side in the prison shops. They were not allowed to talk, but at least they had the comfort of human companionship. The Auburn Prison was run under what was called the *congregate* (together) *and silent system.*

Everyday Life: Reform in America, copyright © Good Year Books

Another method of treating prisoners was started at the Western Penitentiary of Pennsylvania in 1828. It was called the *separate and silent system.* Here each prisoner was kept in a large cell divided into two parts. One part served as living quarters. The other functioned as a workplace, where the prisoner performed some kind of handicraft. Attached to each cell was a small

exercise yard. Light entered the prisoner's cell through a small slit in the outer wall. Conversation was limited to the prison official who passed food and other materials through a small door at the front of the cell. In this confined environment, the prisoner spent his or her entire sentence.

Although the separate and silent system was an improvement over the days when prisoners were lumped together in one large cell, it is easy to see that it was not much better than the Quaker method. Prisoner morale and productivity, compared to the congregate and silent system, remained low. For some reason, however, the western Pennsylvania method was the one adopted by most European countries in the 19th century.

In the United States, the Auburn system of keeping prisoners in individual cells during the night but permitting them to congregate by day became the preferred method. Major prisons, such as Sing Sing in New York, all followed this policy. And, although silence among prisoners continued to be the rule, this requirement began to give way in the 1930s.

Other reforms quickly followed. Among these were points for good behavior, educating prisoners for life after their release, and early parole. A major reform concerned the treatment of juveniles. States began to build reformatories, which are special prisons for young offenders. The goal of reformatories is to change behavior and prepare juveniles for a life free of crime once they are released.

Many reforms still need to be made in our prison system. Some prisons are overcrowded and wracked by violence and unrest. States have found it necessary to release criminals because there is not sufficient space to keep them confined. Today, prison reform is a major issue confronting government at every level.

Prisoners line up at the State Penitentiary at Auburn, New York. Auburn was the first prison in America to allow contact between inmates during daytime hours. From an 1842 wood engraving.

Name _____ Date _____

Recall Information You Have Read

Without looking back over the chapter, write your best answers to these questions.

1. What role did Dorothea Dix play in the Civil War?

_____

_____

_____

2. How were mentally ill people treated before Dorothea Dix brought about much-needed reforms? Give examples.

_____

_____

_____

3. What kind of prison reform was urged by the Quakers in the late 18th century?

_____

_____

_____

4. Distinguish between the congregate and silent and the separate and silent systems of prison administration.

_____

_____

_____

5. What is a reformatory, and what is its purpose?

_____

_____

_____

 *Everyday Life: Reform in America,* copyright © Good Year Books

Name _____ Date _____

Complete a Prison Questionnaire

Below are statements having to do with prisons and the treatment of inmates. Indicate whether you agree or disagree by circling the appropriate response at the beginning of each. On the lines provided, explain why you feel as you do.

(Agree/Disagree) 1. All prisoners should be required to serve their full terms without any chance of early release.

_____

_____

_____

(Agree/Disagree) 2. Prison life should be made so harsh and uncomfortable that every inmate would vow never to return upon being released.

_____

_____

_____

(Agree/Disagree) 3. Prisoners should be permitted to "go on strike" to obtain more privileges and better conditions.

_____

_____

_____

(Agree/Disagree) 4. The criminal justice system is too easy on juvenile offenders.

_____

_____

_____

(Agree/Disagree) 5. States should house criminals in tents to alleviate the problem of prison overcrowding.

_____

_____

_____

Name _____ Date _____

Solve a Dorothea Dix Puzzle

Fill in the sentences for clues to complete the puzzle about Dorothea Dix.

```
_  _  _  D  _
_  _  _  O  _  _
_  _  _  R  _  _  _
   _  O  _  _  _  _  _  _
_  _  _  T  _  _  _  _
   _  H  _  _  _  _
   _  E  _  _  _  _  _
   _  A  _  _  _
      D  _  _  _
      I  _  _
   _  X
```

1. Dorothea Dix's middle name was _____.

2. In 1854, Dorothea Dix traveled to _____ to help the mentally ill.

3. During the Civil War, Dorothea Dix served as Superintendent of _____.

4. Dorothea was _____ years old when she became a teacher.

5. While in England, Dorothea had an audience with Queen _____.

6. Dorothea required that all nurses under her supervision had to be at least _____ years of age.

7. Dorothea Dix began her career as a _____.

8. Dorothea Dix was responsible for having the first asylum for the mentally ill constructed in the Asian nation of _____.

9. Dorothea Dix and others worked to end the practice of imprisoning people for _____.

10. Dorothea Dix is best known for her work with the mentally _____.

11. While in Europe, Dorothea Dix discussed reform with Pope Pius ____.

Everyday Life: Reform in America, copyright © Good Year Books

Chapter 4 • *Prisons and Asylums*

Name _____ Date _____

Name Those Synonyms

The following words are taken from the chapter you have just read. Write two synonyms for each on the lines provided.

1. wrath (n) _____ _____

2. strict (adj) _____ _____

3. cardinal (adj) _____ _____

4. abolished (v) _____ _____

5. standards (n) _____ _____

6. reform (v) _____ _____

7. custom (n) _____ _____

8 confined (v) _____ _____

9. indifferent (adj) _____ _____

10. plight (n) _____ _____

11. expose (v) _____ _____

12. convinced (v) _____ _____

13. petitioned (v) _____ _____

14. solitary (adj) _____ _____

15. modified (v) _____ _____

16. system (n) _____ _____

17. special (adj) _____ _____

18. major (adj) _____ _____

19. release (v) _____ _____

20. encountered (v) _____ _____

Everyday Life: Reform in America, copyright © Good Year Books

33

CHAPTER 5

The Temperance Crusade

I'll drink to that," slurred the drunkard as he raised his glass in another toast.

"You'll drink to anything!" replied his companion of the moment.

The above gag has been used countless times by comedians and others in the entertainment world. But the two lines of which it is composed go far to explain the attitude of Americans toward drink in the early days of our nation.

From the beginning, the colonists developed the habit of drinking beer or ale with their meals. They had to, for water was often unfit for consumption. They also viewed "drinking a toast" on certain occasions as a time-honored tradition that caused nobody any harm. The problem was that many Americans began to use any event or occurrence as a reason to uncork the bottle.

Frederick Marryat, a British writer, wrote about American drinking habits in 1839. He said Americans drank when they met and drank when they parted. They drank when they quarreled and drank when they made up. If they won an election, they drank and celebrated; if they lost, they drank and swore. They began drinking in the morning and continued until night. According to Marryat, the average American's opinion of water was that "it was very good for navigation."

Marryat, of course, was stretching things a bit. All Americans did not drink from sunrise to sunset, but many of them did. The situation became so bad that by the 1830s reformers were calling for the complete abolition of alcoholic beverages. They based their demand on the fact that records showed a high correlation between alcohol and crime. They also pointed to the effect of alcoholism on family life. A large number of battered and bruised women convinced reformers nationwide that liquor had to go.

Although years passed before any connection was made between alcohol and health, reformers found others reasons to attack "Demon Rum." The fact that some were not true did not lessen their impact. One commonly-held belief was that alcohol caused insanity. Another was that alcohol made the body combustible and likely to burst into flames at any moment!

Captain Frederick Marryat, a British novelist and naval officer who found American drinking habits both unusual and amusing.

CAPTAIN MARRYAT, R.N. C.B.

Everyday Life: Reform in America, copyright © Good Year Books

The attack on alcohol gained momentum with the founding of the United States Temperance Union in 1833. *Temperance* is a word that means "being moderate in actions, speech, and habits." Reformers applied the term to their effort to control the sale and consumption of alcoholic drinks. Attempts to instill self-control in imbibers (drinkers) soon mushroomed into a campaign to outlaw alcohol completely. Temperance leaders asked people to sign pledges promising they would either stop drinking or never begin. Many did.

In 1846, Maine became the first state to ban the making and selling of liquor. Some twelve other states followed. But passing a law forbidding something and actually enforcing it are two different things. In some places, no attempt was made to uphold the ban. As a result, lecturers began to travel about speaking on the evils of consuming alcohol. One was an Irish priest named Father Mathew. Another, and the most sensational of the anti-alcohol lecturers, was a reformed drunkard named John B. Gough.

Gough was an Englishmen who came to America in 1831 to seek his fortune. Going from one job to another and not succeeding at any, he sought escape by drinking. His luck changed temporarily when, because he had some talent as a ventriloquist and comic, he landed a job with an acting company. But when the company went bankrupt, Gough was once again unemployed and back on the bottle.

John Gough's life changed one night when he happened to attend a meeting of reformed alcoholics. As he stood to tell his personal story, his natural talent for acting came through. He held the others in attendance spellbound as he enacted his confession in a most theatrical way. Almost overnight, there was a demand for his testimony at other gatherings. Gough, quickly realizing that money could be made from the misfortunes of others, polished his presentation and hit the temperance trail.

John Gough, a reformed alcoholic, whose ventriloquist skills added to his effectiveness as a lecturer. His performances convinced many to sign pledges to never drink again.

For 40 years, Gough traveled throughout America and England lecturing people on the evils and pitfalls of drink. In his first year alone he traveled almost 7,000 miles and gave nearly 400 speeches. While "performing," he frightened listeners with horror stories of drunkards. He glared and growled. He rolled on the floor and trembled. His ventriloquist ability allowed him to

play the roles of alcoholic and reformer alike. His act was quite effective. During his many years on the temperance tour, he succeeded in getting several thousand reformed alcoholics to sign pledges that they would never drink again.

The drive to ban alcohol intensified in the years following the Civil War. Between 1869 and 1893, three organizations were founded that led the way.

Ladies of the Women's Temperance Union smash barrels of liquor at a railroad depot in Indiana.

The first was the Prohibition Party, which appeared in 1869. It entered national politics in 1872 and 20 years later polled 271,000 votes. As recently as 1960, it received more than 46,000 votes in the national election.

The second organization was the Woman's Christian Temperance Union, which was founded in Cleveland, Ohio, in 1874. It quickly had chapters nationwide, and, like the Prohibition Party, fought to abolish the manufacture and sale of all liquor. One of its most energetic members was Carry Nation, of whom more is written later in this chapter.

The third temperance organization was the Anti-Saloon League, formed in 1893. It became a force in politics by supporting only those candidates who favored prohibition. Both the Woman's Christian Temperance Union and the Anti-Saloon League were well-financed by voluntary contributions.

In spite of the temperance efforts, Americans continued to drink. They even got clever in disguising it. During the 1880s, a company called the Vinous Rubber Grape Company put out a product that became popular with some imbibers. It consisted of a variety of "grapes" filled with liquor encased in a rubber skin. The user bit down on the grape, which burst and ejected the liquor into the mouth. He or she then discarded the skin. The Vinous Rubber Grape Company's product was said to be especially popular with opera-goers and sleigh riders.

By the time Americans began indulging in liquor-filled grapes, some temperance reformers had had enough. One such person was Carry A. Nation. She became the best-known of all temperance crusaders, primarily because of the violent approach she took to close saloons and end the sale of alcohol. Many praised her efforts. Others saw her as intolerant and not a little

Everyday Life: Reform in America, copyright © Good Year Books

obnoxious. In addition to her crusade against alcohol, she also campaigned against the use of tobacco and what she saw as the revealing clothing worn by the women of her day. With regard to tobacco, she often walked the streets snatching cigarettes and cigars from the mouths of smokers.

In 1889, Carry Nation moved to Kansas with her second husband, David Nation. (Her first husband was a drunkard who died soon after their marriage.) Immediately upon arriving in the small Kansas town of Medicine Lodge, she noticed that the law banning the sale of alcohol in the state was not enforced. Medicine Lodge had seven saloons, and all of them openly sold liquor.

Carry Nation decided to do something about it. With a small gathering of followers, she began to preach and pray at the entrance to Medicine Lodge's saloons. She kept up the pressure on owners, even standing in church on Sundays and mentioning their names. After a few months, every saloon in town had closed its doors.

Carry Nation was just getting warmed up. In June 1899, she claimed she had a vision telling her to go to the town of Kiowa and smash (literally) the saloons there. She loaded her buggy with stones and set out to fulfill her mission. After wrecking several bars in the town, she dared local officials to arrest her. They declined.

Armed with hatchet and Bible, reformer Carry Nation prepares to swing into action. Her violent campaign against alcoholic drink won her nationwide notoriety.

From rocks and stones, Carry Nation soon graduated to what became her symbol: the hatchet. In the next few years, she traveled throughout Kansas wrecking saloons and smashing kegs of alcohol with her trusty weapon. When she moved into other states that permitted drinking, she was often arrested and sometimes beaten. But nothing deterred her from what she considered her personal calling. She even thought that her name, "carry a nation," was symbolic of her mission.

Through the efforts of Carry Nation and others, the 18th Amendment banning the manufacture and sale of alcoholic beverages became part of the Constitution in 1919. It remained in effect until 1933, when it was repealed by the 21st Amendment. After 14 years of prohibition, Americans realized that the ban on alcohol had created more problems than it had solved. But that is another story that is addressed in your history text or in a book dealing with the Constitution.

Name _____ Date _____

Use Your Critical-Thinking Skills

Write your best answers to the questions shown.

1. What health problems are associated with the excessive use of alcohol?

   _____
   _____
   _____

2. What social problems are brought about by the abuse of alcohol? Name as many as you can.

   _____
   _____
   _____

3. Was Carry Nation right or wrong in taking the law into her own hands in attacking saloons? Would you have done the same? Why or why not? Is violence or breaking the law ever justified in righting a wrong? Why or why not?

   _____
   _____
   _____

4. In your opinion, why do some young people start experimenting with drugs such as alcohol and tobacco? What advice would you give to a friend who was considering doing the same?

   _____
   _____
   _____

Name _____ Date _____

Create a Poster

Using a variety of colored pencils, pens, and markers for effect, create a poster designed to influence young people not to become involved in alcohol, tobacco, or other drugs. Either draw an illustration of your own or select an appropriate picture from a magazine.

Name _____ Date _____

Distinguish Between Fact and Opinion

Many times people say things they believe to be true. In reality they may be only stating an opinion. It is often difficult to distinguish between fact and opinion.

Carefully read the statements about alcohol on this page. Then, on the blank line before each, indicate whether you think it is a fact or an opinion. Mark **F** for fact and **O** for opinion.

_____1. Alcohol is a drug.

_____2. Drinking makes a person more socially acceptable.

_____3. Excessive use of alcohol can affect one's ability to concentrate or memorize.

_____4. Alcoholism is a disease.

_____5. Alcohol provides a person with permanent relief from his or her problems.

_____6. A drastic reduction in teenage drinking would occur if convenience stores and supermarkets were forbidden to sell beer and wine.

_____7. Young people who drink are more mature than those who do not.

_____8. Alcohol poses health problems for people who use it.

_____9. One or two drinks have no effect on one's ability to safely drive an automobile.

_____10. An alcoholic drinks because he or she must.

_____11. Most alcoholics are persons of bad character and questionable morals.

_____12. Alcoholism may affect people of any race or economic status.

_____13. It is against the law for adults to purchase alcoholic beverages for anyone under the age of 21.

_____14. The primary responsibility for teaching young people about the dangers of alcohol rests with our nation's schools.

Everyday Life: Reform in America, copyright © Good Year Books

Name _____ Date _____

Interpret a Line Graph

Some people fool themselves into believing that one or two drinks have little effect on their ability to function normally. They also think that the alcohol in beer, whiskey, and other such beverages stays in the body for only a short period of time.

The graph on this page shows the relationship between the number of drinks taken and the time for the alcohol to leave the body. By way of explanation, one drink refers to $1\frac{1}{2}$ ounces of whiskey, $5\frac{1}{2}$ ounces of wine, or two cans or bottles of beer.

Using the information on the graph, answer these questions.

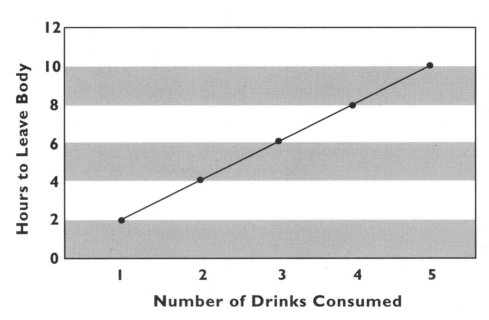

1. For every drink taken, the time required for the effects to wear off increases by _____ hours.

2. Based on the graph, a person who consumed 12 drinks would require _____ hours for the alcohol to leave his or her body.

3. If a cocktail contains $1\frac{1}{2}$ ounces of whiskey, a person drinking eight would consume _____ ounces of strong liquor.

4. From looking at the graph, what can one conclude about the relationship between the number of drinks consumed and the time required for the effects to wear off?

CHAPTER 6

Child Labor

I magine it is the year 1911. Also imagine that you are five years old and that your mother has awakened you to go to work. It is two o'clock in the morning. You and your mother must be at the cannery by three to begin peeling the shells off iced shrimp. You eat what happens to be in the house at the time and set off in the darkness. You are only five, but you have followed the same routine for more than a year.

Sound unbelievable? Children four and sometimes younger working at full-time jobs? What about their parents? What were they thinking at the time? Why would they permit such a thing to happen? These and other questions are probably racing through your mind at the moment.

The answer to your questions lies in the attitude toward children for many years.

Until well into the 20th century, children were seen as small adults. Their clothing was modeled after that of adults, and they were expected to behave as such. There was little time reserved for childhood. Many people thought work kept children occupied and out of trouble. At least some factory owners considered children laboring away at machines or at some other workplace a "beautiful sight." In addition, many families needed the extra money a child worker could add to the family income.

Child labor in America dates from the 18th century. In 1781, a man named Samuel Slater opened a textile mill in Rhode Island. As was the custom at the time, he hired young children to run his spinning machines. Some sources say that by 1801 some 100 children aged 4 to 10 worked in Slater's mill.

The labor of children was preferred over that of adults for several reasons. First, children could be hired at a cheaper rate. Second, they were not as likely as adult workers to cause trouble. Third, their tiny hands were better suited to working around machinery. Spinning machines were even made with small fingers in mind. The fact that many of these small fingers got mangled in the constantly moving machines never bothered the average factory owner. By the 1830s, 40 percent of the mill workers in New England were children.

Children in a textile factory labor under the watchful eye of a foreman. Workdays of more than 12 hours were commonplace for children at the time.

Everyday Life: Reform in America, copyright © Good Year Books

Because the factory system began in the textile mills of England, so too did the use of child labor to operate the spinning machines. Conditions there were much worse than they ever became in the United States. English factory owners collected pauper children from poorhouses and worked them without pay. Impoverished parents also sent their children to work in the mills for the few pennies they could earn. Such unfortunate little ones, some as young as five, had to work up to 16 hours a day. Often they were chained to their machines.

Although they were not chained, child laborers in America nevertheless suffered at the hands of their employers. They worked long hours under dangerous and unhealthy conditions. They received no breaks and had no time for fresh air or play. If they nodded or tried to rest a moment at their task, they could expect to be rapped with a broom handle or some other object.

In the cotton mills that sprang up in the South after the Civil War, boys and girls were often splashed with water to keep them awake at their machines. Few people seemed to really care about the plight of these children, not even when young girls were patted or touched inappropriately by calloused foremen. Many years passed before various states enacted laws to end the worst abuses that occurred in these workplaces. Many more years passed before the federal government took action.

Young spinner at work in a Carolina cotton mill in 1908. How old do you think the little girl might be?

A tour of America at the turn of the 20th century would have revealed children working at every imaginable job. Young boys especially were hired to perform tasks that were both dangerous and harmful to their health. One of the worst places where boys as young as nine worked was in the breakers of the coal mines of western Pennsylvania. Here many of them either suffered terrible injuries or developed asthma or tuberculosis from years of breathing coal dust. Some of them were even killed.

The breakers was a building where large chunks of coal were broken into smaller pieces before being cleaned and washed. On the way to the washer, the coal passed along a chute over which young boys sat hunched for as long as 12 hours a day. Their job was to reach into the chute and pick out pieces of

A group of breaker boys photographed at a coal mine about the year 1900. Poor health, injuries, and sometimes death resulted from the terrible conditions under which they worked.

slate from the coal as it passed by. If they grew tired or were not alert, they sometimes got their fingers caught in the machinery that moved the chute along. More than one fell into the chute itself, to be carried away and suffocated under mounds of coal and coal dust.

Other children—both boys and girls—worked in canneries and on farms. It was not unusual to find children as young as three shucking oysters or working in a field. Others polished shoes or sold newspapers on the street. Still others labored from dawn to night in home sweatshops, helping their parents make such things as artificial flowers and cigars. No sooner were some children past the toddler stage than they were put to work.

A large number of child laborers were the children of immigrant parents. Perhaps that is why it took so many years for government at both the local and the national level to take action. Few Americans concerned themselves with what was or was not happening with the children of immigrants. Even when states passed child labor laws, they were often not enforced.

The first child labor laws were passed in New England. In 1813, Connecticut enacted legislation requiring that working children must have some formal schooling. Twenty-three years later, in 1836, Massachusetts passed a law stating that children under 15 had to go to school 3 months a year. These were, to be sure, not far-reaching laws, but they at least were a beginning.

In the 1880s, America's labor unions took up the cause of children in the workplace. Both the Knights of Labor and its successor, the American Federation of Labor (AFL), called on states to outlaw child labor altogether. This did not occur, but the efforts of the unions were partially successful. By 1899, 28 states had passed laws regulating some aspects of child labor.

At the turn of the century, reformers began to work for a national child labor law to support those passed by some states. The National Child Labor Committee was formed in 1904 with this purpose in mind. One of the committee's more effective employees was Lewis Hine, who quit his job as a schoolteacher to become an investigative photographer. It was Hine more

than anyone who called the nation's attention to the evils associated with child labor. His shocking pictures of working children in every kind of environment caused Americans to demand that the system be ended.

In his work for the National Child Labor Committee, Lewis Hine traveled the length and breadth of America. He photographed children working in the mills of New England and the South. He captured on film the hopelessness on the faces of the boys who worked in the breakers of the western Pennsylvania mine fields. He snapped pictures of three- and four-year-olds laboring in canneries and in fields from New Jersey to California. He took photographs of children working in home sweatshops or selling newspapers on busy street corners. If children were employed anywhere, Hine was there clicking away with his camera.

A young farm worker at the turn of the 20th century. Reformers discovered children as young as three working long hours in America's fields.

Results at the national level came slowly. Finally, President Theodore Roosevelt (1901–1909) urged Congress to pass a national child labor law. Senator William E. Borah introduced such a bill in the Senate in 1916, pointing out that "the government should do for children what it has already done for calves and pigs!"

But then a funny thing happened. Congress dutifully passed the law, only to have it declared unconstitutional by the Supreme Court. A similar law passed in 1919 was also struck down by the justices of the Court. Their logic? In their opinion, a national child labor law interfered with a child's right to work!

It was not until 1938 that the problem of child labor was successfully addressed by the federal government. In that year, the Fair Labor Standards Act set a minimum age of 16 for children who worked full time. Those who had after-school jobs had to be 14, and any young person whose job was considered dangerous had to be 18. With this act, more than 150 years of loosely regulated child labor in America came to an end.

Name _____ Date _____

Solve Some Child-Labor Math Problems

Child laborers in America worked incredibly long hours for a mere pittance (small amount of money). Employers got by with paying them low wages because they were children and because there were no government agencies to look out for their welfare.

On this page are four word problems dealing with child labor. Work each problem in the space provided, and write its correct answer on the accompanying line.

1. Nikita is a young Russian boy working in the breakers building of a coal mine. He works 12 hours a day, 6 days a week, and is paid 5 cents an hour. How many hours does he need to work to earn $60.00? (Helpful hint: Review ratio in your mathematics book.)

_____ hours

2. Tommy began working at a glass factory for 40 cents a day. If he works every night from 5:30 P.M. to 3:30 A.M., what is his hourly wage?

_____ an hour

3. Gina is a seven-year-old girl who works with her parents in a tenement sweatshop. She averages earning 90 cents a week, while her parents together earn $8.10. What percent of the total family weekly income does Gina earn?

_____ percent

4. Pearl is a ten-year old girl who works in a textile mill in South Carolina. Her total pay for a six-day work week is $3.00. Browsing through a Sears, Roebuck catalogue one Sunday, she gazes longingly at things she wishes she could buy. If her income was not needed to help support her family, how many days' income would she need to buy the items below?

Girl's Gingham Dress $2.25

Coat $3.25

Pair of Strap Sandals ....$ .88

_____ days

Everyday Life: Reform in America, copyright © Good Year Books

Name _____ Date _____

Write a Letter to the President

Imagine you are your present age but living in the year 1905. Write a letter to President Theodore Roosevelt asking that he urge Congress to pass a national law outlawing child labor in the United States. Give as many reasons as you can why you think child labor is wrong.

September 23, 1905

The President
The White House
Washington, D.C.

Dear Mr. President:

_____

_____

_____

_____

_____

_____

_____

_____

_____

_____

_____

_____

_____

_____

_____

_____

_____

_____

Sincerely,

_____

Name _____ Date _____

Dramatize an Event

Divide the class into groups and have each choose one of the skits below. Students should use their imagination and creative skills in planning their skit, which should be about five minutes in length.

Students not participating directly in a skit can make simple props and costumes or critique and rate the skits at the conclusion of the activity. There is a lead-in to each skit to help students in their planning.

Skit 1—Parents Discussing Whether to Send Their Son to Work in the Breakers of a Coal Mine

Immigrant families who migrated to the coal fields of western Pennsylvania often had no choice but to put their young children to work. Center this skit around a husband and wife weighing the pros and cons of having their nine-year-old son work in a coal mine.

Skit 2—Lewis Hine Talking to a Ten-Year Old Girl Working in a Southern Cotton Mill

You have learned that Lewis Hine was an investigative photographer for the National Child Labor Committee, and as such visited and made pictures of children at work across America. Center this skit around a dialogue that might have taken place between Hine and a young girl employee of a cotton mill.

Skit 3—Members of the House of Representatives Debating the Passage of a National Child Labor Law

You have also learned that legislation regulating child labor was slow in coming to America. In this skit, have congressmen debate whether such a law is necessary and what it should entail.

Skit 4—Several Factory Owners Discussing the Merits of Child Labor

Most Americans saw nothing wrong with young children laboring in the workplace. They even thought there were benefits to be derived from youngsters working long hours in factories and other places.

Center this skit around a dialogue that might have taken place among several factory owners as they discuss the issue of child labor.

Everyday Life: Reform in America, copyright © Good Year Books

Name _____ Date _____

Prepare a Time-Machine Journal

Imagine that Isabel, a nine-year-old textile mill worker of the early 1900s, has been transported by a time machine to the year 1999. On the lines provided, compose a journal describing her thoughts and experiences as she finds herself on a school playground with others her age who are happily engaged in play.

Date _____

Dear Journal,

CHAPTER 7

Other Social Reforms

Even before Lewis Hine helped expose Americans to the evils of child labor, a young Danish immigrant in New York City was doing the same for slums. His name was Jacob A. Riis.

Jacob Riis came to America in 1870. For more than 20 years he worked as a police reporter for two New York City newspapers. During his career, he covered and wrote about crime, corruption, and vice in the slums of the big city. In 1890, he wrote a book entitled *How the Other Half Lives*. It shocked America and led to much-needed reforms in slums nationwide.

Riis made Americans aware of the misery and unsanitary conditions associated with life in large city tenements. (Tenements are buildings divided into many sets of rooms or apartments.) In *How the Other Half Lives*, Riis wrote of four-to-five story buildings in which 16 to 20 families—mostly immigrants—lived. Each family was crammed into no more than three tiny rooms. Sometimes as many as nine or more persons lived in one room. It was not uncommon for parents to sleep on the floor and their children in boxes. If there was a baby in the family, it often slept in a shawl suspended by cords from the rafters of the ceiling.

One hundred or more persons might occupy one run-down tenement. Riis found that in one block of Manhattan there were 2,781 persons crowded into dirty and unsafe apartments. Some buildings had only one bathroom to serve all its occupants. Tenants had to line up to wash and take care of bodily functions. Many times the toilet in the bathroom was stopped up and incapable of being flushed. Inconvenience and uncleanliness only added to other miseries suffered by the poor occupants of these slum tenements.

A visitor to a crowded tenement was stunned by what he or she saw. Roaches and rats scurried about everywhere; trash and garbage littered stairways and halls. Pipes froze in the winter and spewed water everywhere when they thawed. Some buildings were unheated and nearly all were dimly lit. In the midst of such filth and discomfort, little children lived, played, and

Jacob Riis, Danish-born journalist and reformer. His book, *How the Other Half Lives*, shocked Americans and led to legislation that corrected the worst abuses associated with big-city slums.

died. Disease was rampant; one figure placed the tuberculosis rate among tenement dwellers at 34 percent.

With regard to small children, Riis discovered that many were left alone to fend for themselves while their parents worked. Others were left in the care of older sisters who were often no more than babies themselves. It is not surprising that many children, unsupervised and deprived of life's barest necessities, drifted into a world of vice and crime as they grew older.

Lewis Hine's photograph of ramshackle wooden tenements in Washington, D.C., in 1908. In addition to the health threats they posed, such buildings were notorious fire traps.

Through the efforts of Jacob Riis and other social reformers, laws were passed that corrected the worst slum conditions. A 1901 New York City ordinance required better ventilation, sanitation, and fire protection for tenements. Earlier, the city had passed another law prohibiting rooms without windows. Slowly the worst health and safety hazards associated with slums were addressed.

Jacob Riis also led the fight for school and city playgrounds. By 1910, over 150 American cities had playgrounds. Many were little more than sand lots, but they served the purpose. Playgrounds were especially important in slum areas where poor immigrant families congregated. Before playgrounds, children played in alleys or on dirty stairwells, surrounded by garbage and rats. Playgrounds not only provided immigrant children with fresh air and exercise but gave them much-needed breaks from the monotony and miseries of slum life.

One year before Jacob Riis published *How the Other Half Lives*, Jane Addams opened Hull House, a settlement house in Chicago. A settlement house is a place in an underprivileged area that offers assistance and services to the poor. Hull House was not the first of such establishments (the University Settlement in New York City that opened in 1886 preceded it), but it by far was the most famous.

Jane Addams started out wanting to be a doctor. Poor health, however, prevented her from entering medical school. In hopes of recovery, her wealthy parents sent her to Europe. It was in London that Jane visited Toynbee Hall,

Jane Addams reads to children at Hull House, one of the first settlement houses in America. Ms. Addams was also very active in the world peace movement.

one of the world's best-known settlement houses. Impressed by what she saw, she returned to America determined to do something similar to help the poor.

Jane and a friend, Ellen Starr, rented a rundown house in the middle of Chicago's slum district. They called it Hull House, after the family that had once owned it. They cleaned and painted and in short time had the old house looking beautiful. They bought furniture, pictures, and plenty of books. In 1889, they opened their settlement house to all who would come.

Hull House quickly became a haven for Chicago's immigrants. With the help of volunteers and other social workers, Miss Addams started a variety of programs and activities to help immigrants better adjust to life in America. Working men could stop there everyday for a nourishing lunch. Working mothers could leave their children in Miss Addam's day nursery, knowing they were in safe hands. Any immigrant interested in taking a class in painting, music, or acting could find all three at Hull House. They could also play games, listen to poetry readings, or work out in a gymnasium. Above all, they could learn English and even take college courses.

Immigrants of every ethnic and religious group came to Hull House. All were welcome: Jews, Poles, Italians, Russians, Germans, Greeks, Hungarians. If they were poor and new to America, there was a place for them. How many received help from Miss Addams and her associates? That number would be almost impossible to determine. But many of those who received help returned years later to thank Miss Addams and to have their children meet her. She was a woman widely loved.

Hull House paved the way for the founding of other settlement houses. South End House was established in Boston in 1891 by Robert A. Woods, another well-known social reformer. Woods called even more attention to the problems of urban areas in his book *The City Wilderness*, which he published in 1898.

At about the same time that South End House opened in Boston, Lillian Wald founded the Henry Street Settlement in New York City. She gained fame in 1902 by starting the first public school nursery service in the world. She also was largely responsible for the founding of the U.S. Children's Bureau in 1912. Like Jane Addams and other reformers, she later became active in the women's suffrage movement.

Another social reformer of note was Graham Taylor. In 1894 he founded a second settlement house in Chicago, which he called the Chicago Commons. Graham had been a pastor until he became a professor of social economics in 1892 at the Chicago Theological Seminary.

But back to Jane Addams. She is probably the best example of a social reformer whose activities covered a wide range of causes. In addition to settlement houses, she strove to improve the lot of children and women workers. She helped bring about some of the first state child labor laws and campaigned for an eight-hour law for working women. Among her other causes were housing reform and adult education for immigrants. She also was responsible for the establishment of the first juvenile court in the United States.

What is often overlooked in textbooks about Jane Addams is her work to promote peace. She was a devoted pacifist who was president of the Woman's International League for Peace and Freedom from 1915–1929. She also served as chairman of the Woman's Peace Party. In 1931, her hard work was recognized when she was awarded the Nobel Prize for peace.

The list of reformers who helped bring about social change is too long to include in this book. But two others of note were Charles Loring Brace and Josephine Shaw Lowell. Charles Loring Brace was a pioneer in child welfare who established the Children's Aid Society of New York in 1853. Josephine Shaw Lowell (1843–1905) was a social reformer who helped found the New York Charity Organization Society. She also introduced important reforms in hospitals, asylums, and prisons. In that respect, she was something akin to a latter-day Dorothea Dix.

Lillian Wald, a pioneer in public health nursing. She established the first public school nursery service at her Henry Street Settlement in New York.

Everyday Life: Reform in America, copyright © Good Year Books

Name _____ Date _____

Interpret a Picture

Jacob Riis took many pictures depicting life in New York's slums. Look at the photograph of a young girl holding a toddler, and write answers to the questions at the bottom of the page.

1. What do you think the relationship is between the girl and the baby?

   _____

2. What responsibility has probably been assigned to the girl?

   _____

3. Look closely at the girl's face. Is she sad? Happy? Pensive (thoughtful)?

   _____

4. What do you think the girl is thinking?

   _____

5. What does the condition of the door and other parts of the building suggest about the kind of place where the girl lives?

   _____

   _____

Everyday Life: Reform in America, copyright © Good Year Books.

Name _____ Date _____

Complete a Reformer Puzzle

ACROSS

2. Jane Addams won the Nobel _____ Prize.

4. Jane Addams' first choice of careers.

5. Ellen _____, friend of Jane Addams.

8. Disease often contracted by immigrants.

10. Rodent invaders of tenements.

12. Where Toynbee Hall was located.

13. Where Hull House was located.

14. Large building divided into many apartments.

15. Charles _____ Brace, founder of the Children's Aid Society.

DOWN

1. U.S. Children's _____.

3. Jane _____, famous social reformer

6. _____ House, Jane Addams' settlement house.

7. Where South End House was located.

9. Jacob A. _____.

11. Lewis _____, famous photographer.

12. Josephine Shaw _____, a social reformer.

Name _____ Date _____

Use Context Clues to Complete Sentence

Use the words from the word box to fill in the blanks in the sentences telling a story from Jane Addams' childhood.

accompanying	green	stood
beside	later	success
born	people	sympathy
children	play	traveled
father	shocked	wanted
fortunate	someday	years

Jane Addams was _____ in the little village of Cedarville, Illinois, in 1860. Her _____ owned a flour mill, and his _____ at business made the family quite well-off. As a result, Jane never _____ for anything as a child.

In spite of living in comfort, young Jane Addams felt _____ for people less _____ than she. One day, while _____ her father to his mill, their carriage _____ through a poor part of town. Jane was _____ by the run-down houses she saw. She was troubled by the fact that the houses _____ right at the edge of the sidewalk. There were no yards or _____ grass anywhere. Where did the _____ who lived in those houses play?

Sitting _____ her father in the carriage, Jane turned and told him that _____ she would buy a big house and open it up to poor _____. That way, little children would have a place to _____.

At the time, little Jane was only seven _____ old. But, true to her word, she bought and opened Hull House in Chicago 22 years _____. Not only did poor children then have a place to play and to seek comfort, their parents had a place that offered them help and advice in adjusting to life in America.

Everyday Life: Reform in America, copyright © Good Year Books

Name _____ Date _____

Answer Questions About Tuberculosis

You have learned that immigrants who lived in overcrowded tenements were highly susceptible to tuberculosis. In your science textbook or an encyclopedia, research tuberculosis and then answer the questions.

1. What was another name people formerly used for tuberculosis?

   _____

2. What causes tuberculosis?

   _____

3. How is tuberculosis spread from one person to another?

   _____

4. What are the symptoms of tuberculosis?

   _____

   _____

   _____

   _____

   _____

5. List several ways in which tuberculosis is detected.

   _____

6. How is tuberculosis treated?

   _____

   _____

7. Can tuberculosis be prevented or contained? If so, how?

   _____

   _____

8. Has tuberculosis been eliminated in the United States?

   _____

CHAPTER 8

Labor Unions

Until the end of the 18th century, all goods produced in America were made by craftsmen either at home or in small shops. Each craftsman was his own boss, setting his own hours and work pace. He took pride in good handicraft and felt a sense of accomplishment in what he created with his hands.

The craftsman was free to do as he chose. If he wanted to work from dawn to dusk, he did. If he chose to work from eight to noon, that was his personal decision. If he wanted to take a day off and go fishing, he could do that too. There was no one around to tell him what he could or could not do.

All this changed with the coming of the factory system. With machines capable of turning out goods much faster, the craftsman waned in importance. To survive, he had to take a low-paying job in a factory operating a machine that required no skill and that gave him no personal satisfaction. He worked long hours at starvation wages under the worst possible conditions. If he complained, he was simply fired and another worker took his place. He had no place to turn for help.

Not all craftsmen, to be sure, were forced into factories as a result of the Industrial Revolution. There were still individual tradesmen such as carpenters and printers who continued to work for themselves. It was these craftsmen who started the labor movement in America in the 1820s. By 1830, most of the major crafts had formed what were called "trade societies" to look after their interests. These associations resembled the guilds of the Middle Ages. They paid for members' funerals and took care of families during strikes and hard times.

During the 1830s, trade societies in various cities formed citywide groups and began working together to improve their lot. They succeeded in attaining a 10-hour workday for all craftsmen working on government projects, such as dams and shipyards. They also influenced several states to apply the 10-hour limit to working children. Not the least of their accomplishments was helping to end imprisonment for debt in America.

Some trade societies united into national trade unions. Typographers in 1850 were the first to organize at the

A blacksmith of the early 1800s at work in his shop. Such skilled craftsmen fared better than most workers during the Industrial Revolution.

Everyday Life: Reform in America, copyright © Good Year Books

national level. In the years before the Civil War, some 30 other "nationals" came into existence. They included unions of cigarmakers, stonecutters, and blacksmiths, to name a few. Because members of such unions were skilled tradesmen, they had some success in bargaining with employers.

Not so with factory workers. Because they were unskilled, factory owners could simply fire them if they caused trouble and hire other workers. There were always men and women eager to accept any job at any pay. And then there were children who could be hired for almost nothing.

In spite of the risks, workers sometimes did go out on strike. This meant that they refused to work. When they did, they would picket the factory or place where they were employed. To *picket* means to stand or walk back and forth at the entrance of a workplace, carrying signs and attempting to stop other employees from entering. Such work stoppages, however, were usually unsuccessful. All an employer had to do was call in police or troops, who used guns and clubs to quickly disperse the strikers. In such confrontations, workers were often killed. Brutal put-downs of labor disputes were tolerated because the government sided with the employers. So did most Americans, who viewed unions as conspiracies run by agitators and *socialists* (people who want the government to control factories and other major means of production).

Policemen on horseback and swinging truncheons disperse strikers in Pittsburgh. For years, laws were stacked in favor of employers, and police and soldiers attacking strikers was a common sight.

The first successful labor union at the national level was the Knights of Labor. It was founded in 1869 by Uriah Stephens, a Philadelphia garment cutter. The Knights opened membership to all workers, both skilled and unskilled. A person's race, sex, or kind of job was of no consequence. All were welcomed.

To protect its members from reprisals by employers, the Knights of Labor was at first a secret organization. Some of its practices and rituals may seem amusing to us today. Candidates for membership were taken to a secret location at night, where they took an oath of loyalty while standing in a circle with other members. Leaders had such important-sounding titles as Master Workman, Venerable Sage, and Inside Esquire (was there also an Outside Esquire?). Stephens even devised a system of symbols, passwords, and secret handshakes.

Such secrecy was necessary because factory and business owners made use of blacklists. A blacklist was a list of workers considered to be troublemakers that was circulated among employers. Any person whose name appeared on a list had no chance of getting a job. Workers were forced to sign a yellow-dog contract, an agreement by which they swore not to join a union. Both blacklists and yellow-dog contracts are illegal today.

As mentioned earlier, workers did sometimes strike. The first big strike in America was the Great Railroad Strike of 1877. It began on July 16, 1877, when four railroads in the East cut the pay of their workers. It started in West Virginia and soon spread nationwide. Railroad employees in Pittsburgh, St. Louis, Chicago, San Francisco, and other cities walked off the job.

Violence associated with the Great Railroad Strike of 1877 cost more than a hundred lives and caused the destruction of millions of dollars of railroad property. The strike spread to railroads from New York to California.

Particularly hard hit by the strike was the city of Pittsburgh. When railroad workers there walked off the job, they were joined by thousands of ruffians and unemployed teenagers. Mobs marched through the city, destroying shops and offices. They set fire to the railroad station and two roundhouses (circular buildings used to store and repair locomotives). They also destroyed 2,000 cars and 25 locomotives belonging to the Pennsylvania Railroad.

Local militia were called out to put down the strikes in the East. They were unsuccessful, however, in fighting the mobs. Some were even unwilling to fire on people they considered their own kind. As a result, the governors of Pennsylvania, Maryland, West Virginia, and Ohio asked that federal troops be sent in to quell the riots. President Rutherford Hayes complied, although he felt some sympathy for the striking workers. The president believed that the railroad owners had brought the crisis on themselves by their ruthless tactics. He is supposed to have written in his diary: "Shall the railroads govern the country or shall the people govern the railroads?"

The Great Railroad Strike of 1877 accomplished little. But labor slowly made progress. The Knights of Labor faded from the scene and was replaced as a major union by the American Federation of Labor (AFL) in 1886. Founded by Samuel Gompers, it was an organization for skilled workers only.

For this reason, it was stronger and much more effective than its predecessor.

Gompers urged the various craft unions that made up the AFL to work for higher wages, better hours, and improved working conditions. He fought hard for the federation's right to *collective bargaining*. This means the right of worker representatives to sit down with owners on an equal level and discuss labor problems. He also steered the federation away from politics and social reforms, which went far to convince people that unions were not controlled by socialists and anarchists (radicals who want to do away with all government).

In 1938 a second major union emerged. It began as a committee meeting of eight presidents of major unions

within the AFL. These presidents felt that workers should be organized by industries rather than by crafts and that unskilled as well as skilled workers should have the opportunity to organize. Their ideas led to their unions being expelled from the AFL. In response, they created the CIO, or Congress of Industrial Organizations. Although the AFL and the CIO merged in 1955 to form the AFL-CIO, for 17 years there were two major national unions in the United States.

Because of the work of organized labor, unions in time gained acceptance in the eyes of the government and the public. One of the first breakthroughs was the passage of the Erdman Act in 1898. This act provided for arbitration and mediation in labor disputes. Arbitration refers to arguing sides presenting their case to a mediator, whose decision is then binding on both parties.

Further progress was made in 1913 when the Department of Labor was established. It grew out of the Bureau of Labor, which had been formed in 1884. Also in 1913, Congress passed the Adamson Act, which set an eight-hour workday for railroad workers.

The first major legislation to help workers was the Wagner Act of 1935. It guaranteed workers the right to collective bargaining and defined and outlawed such unfair practices as the blacklist. Three years later, the Wages and Hours Act became a reality. It was the most important labor legislation up to that time. It established the first minimum wage, provided for overtime pay, and brought child labor under control. The 5-day, 40-hour work week to which many Americans have grown accustomed came into being at that time.

Samuel Gompers, who formed the American Federation of Labor in 1886 and served as its president until his death in 1924. His efforts on the part of labor resulted in better wages and working conditions for craft unions.

Name _____ Date _____

Tell Why You Agree or Disagree with These Statements

Here are four statements pertaining to worker/employer relations. In the blank space before each statement, write whether you agree or disagree with the statement. Then on the lines provided, explain why you feel as you do.

1. _____ Workers who strike and interfere with the flow of goods or the carrying out of important services are selfish and self-centered.

_____

_____

_____

2. _____ All employees of the federal government should be allowed to strike.

_____

_____

_____

3. _____ Forcing employers to pay workers a minimum wage is wrong and should be discontinued.

_____

_____

_____

4. _____ The government should never interfere in labor disputes.

_____

_____

_____

Name _____ Date _____

Solve Some Work-Related Math Problems

On this page are four word problems dealing with wages and hours. Solve each in the space provided, and write the correct answer on the blank line.

1. In 1880, Ukrainian-immigrant Nikita S. earned $402.24 for a year's work in the coal mines of Pennsylvania.

   a. What was his average monthly pay? _____

   b. How much did he have left each month after paying 30 percent of his income for rent? (Round your answer) _____

2. The Fair Labor Standards Act of 1938, also known as the Wages and Hours Act, established a minimum wage of 25 cents an hour. If this amount increased 1400 percent by 1990, what was the minimum wage in 1990? _____

3. Jason and Kaylin both work after school at the Hamburger House. They work two hours each afternoon from Monday to Friday and then eight hours on Saturday. They earn $5.15 an hour. What is the total earnings for each per week? _____

4. Robert earns $11.50 an hour for a 40-hour work week. What is his net pay if $92.00 is deducted for income tax and $23.75 for social security? _____

Name _____ Date _____

Write a Letter

Imagine that you, like many Americans, consider today's minimum wage far too low. Write a letter to your Congresswoman, Representative Ima Lawmaker, asking that she urge Congress to increase the amount. Give reasons and facts why you think such an increase is justified.

Date _____

The Honorable Ima Lawmaker
House of Representatives
Washington, D.C.

Madam:

_____

_____

_____

_____

_____

_____

_____

_____

_____

_____

_____

_____

_____

_____

_____

Sincerely,

_____

Name _____ Date _____

Indicate Appropriateness of Pay

Listed below are 20 occupations. Indicate by a check (✔) whether you think each is underpaid, overpaid, or paid fairly. Discuss and compare your ratings with your classmates.

	Underpaid	Overpaid	Paid Fairly
Farmers	_____	_____	_____
Custodians	_____	_____	_____
Professional athletes	_____	_____	_____
Police officers	_____	_____	_____
Lawyers	_____	_____	_____
Schoolteachers	_____	_____	_____
School bus drivers	_____	_____	_____
College coaches	_____	_____	_____
Gas station attendants	_____	_____	_____
Photographers	_____	_____	_____
Appliance repairmen and repairwomen	_____	_____	_____
Psychiatrists	_____	_____	_____
Unskilled laborers	_____	_____	_____
Doctors	_____	_____	_____
Waitresses	_____	_____	_____
Fast-food workers	_____	_____	_____
Firefighters	_____	_____	_____
Postal workers	_____	_____	_____
Airline pilots	_____	_____	_____
Servicemen and servicewomen	_____	_____	_____

Political Reforms

Suppose you had to choose one word to describe politics in the years between the Civil War and the turn of the 20th century. If your teacher gave you a choice of *honest, corrupt, progressive*, or *inefficient*, which would you choose? If you selected *corrupt*, you win a smiling face!

In the political sense, the word *corrupt* means "dishonest." Dishonesty was rampant at every level of government in the latter part of the 19th century. Businessmen bribed members of Congress and state legislatures to obtain rich contracts and laws favorable to their interests. City officials accepted bribes from local contractors and directed tax money into their own bank accounts as well. Even the police and the courts were on the take; a jail release or an acquittal was available to anyone who could pay the price.

There were several reasons why politics had sunk to such a level. One had to do with "machine politics." At the local level, government was often controlled by party "bosses" who wielded tremendous power. Along with a handful of other leaders, these bosses headed party organizations or "machines" that governed politics at city and sometimes even state levels.

They gave favors to people and businesses who supported them and offered bribes to officials who counted the ballots on election day. Often they "stuffed ballot boxes" with fake votes.

How, you might ask, could a political machine get by with "stuffing" a ballot box? The answer is that elections before the latter part of the 19th century were nothing like elections are today. Individual political parties printed their own ballots and then recruited voters to mark them as directed. It was rather easy to have someone vote more than once or to have "deceased voters" cast their ballot. It was also easy to change any ballot that did not meet with the political machine's approval. There was no such thing as the secret ballot that later came into use.

Perhaps the most notorious of the political bosses was William Marcy Tweed. He headed what came to be called the Tweed Ring, gaining control of Tammany Hall, headquarters of the Democratic Party in New York City. From 1865 to 1871, Tweed and his associates stole an estimated

New York politician William Marcy Tweed, known as "Boss" Tweed. He and his Democratic party machine, Tammany Hall, ruthlessly dominated New York City politics in the 1860s.

Everyday Life: Reform in America, copyright © Good Year Books

VOTES

$200 million of city funds. As a state senator, he forced through a new city charter that gave his machine total control over New York's finances. In the process, he bribed everyone from the governor down to the mayor and minor city officials.

How dishonest were Tweed and his partners? A look at the way they handled city contracts provides an answer. Businesses that were awarded projects were instructed to increase their bills by over 100 percent, with the overcharge going directly into the pockets of Tweed and a few others. One of Tweed's most infamous deals concerned the construction of a new courthouse. A building that could have been completed for $3 million ended up costing $11 million! A plasterer was paid $133,000 for two days' work, and the thermometers installed in the building cost $7,500! Chairs and tables did not come any cheaper. For 40 of each, the city paid the astronomical price of $170,729.60!

A late-nineteenth century photograph of Tammany Hall, the building. It was the headquarters of the Democratic Party in New York City.

A second reason why politics was so corrupt in the late 1800s was closely related to the first. It concerned a practice that began during the presidency of President Andrew Jackson and grew worse with succeeding administrations. That practice was known as the *spoils system.* The term originated in 1832 with Senator William L. Marcy of New York. Marcy believed strongly in the rule "to the victor belongs the spoils." In his opinion, the winning candidates in elections were justified in removing officeholders of the defeated party and replacing them with friends and supporters. As a result, able officials were often fired and replaced by persons totally incompetent to handle the tasks entrusted to them.

The spoils system also included much nepotism. Nepotism refers to putting relatives in important positions. Whether said relatives were qualified for such posts was seldom considered. Perhaps the prizewinner when it came to giving government jobs to relatives was President Ulysses S. Grant, who served from 1869–1877. He placed more than 20 of his kin in cushy positions during his stay in the White House. His brother held four government jobs at one time, farming out responsibility for each to lesser officials.

VOTES

Grant may have been a brilliant military commander, but he was a failure as president. Although he was honest to a fault, he was a poor judge of men and character. Many of his appointees turned out to be scoundrels and crooks. His personal secretary lined his own pockets by selling government tax stamps to whiskey makers for only a small part of their value. His Secretary of War made off with money intended for the Indians on reservations. Even his brother-in-law got into the act, raising the price of gold so that his friends could make a huge profit. And these were but three Grant appointees who enriched themselves at government expense. There were a number of others.

One of the first steps in reforming our political system came in 1883 with the passage of the Civil Service Act. Pressed by President Chester A. Arthur, this law created the Civil Service Commission to give examinations to persons interested in government positions. At first the law covered about 15,000 federal jobs. Presidents following Arthur added more jobs to the list as time went on. Today, most federal jobs are filled in this manner. Civil Service examinations have all but ended the spoils system in American politics.

Another important reform was the secret ballot. Until the late 1800s, elections in the United States were handled in such a way that there was no privacy in voting. In colonial times, voting was often done by either voice vote or a show of hands. Later, as previously mentioned, political parties printed their own ballots and always knew the candidates selected by the individual voter. The Australian, or secret, ballot ended this undemocratic practice.

Under the secret ballot system, voters received ballots printed by the government, not by a particular political party. They retired to private voting booths to make their selections, after which they dropped their ballots into a locked box. In time, the introduction of voting machines added even more safeguards to one's right to privacy in voting.

The next important political reform was the direct primary. The word *primary* means "first" and refers to a first election before the general election that follows. Its purpose is to allow voters to select their party's candidates for

Ulysses S. Grant, who excelled as a general but failed as president. His term was marred by political scandals.

VOTES   100   17th Amendment

office. Until 1903, when the direct primary was first used in Wisconsin, candidates were chosen either by party conventions or party bosses. Today, voters in many states can also participate in presidential primaries where they designate their choice for president. Presidential primaries are held every four years before the parties' national conventions. In most cases, delegates to the national conventions are bound to vote for the party candidate who emerged victorious in their state's primary.

An amendment was necessary to bring about a fourth reform. That was the 17th Amendment of 1913, which provided for the direct election of U.S. senators by the people. Up to that time, senators to Congress were chosen by state legislatures. This arrangement worked fine while America was small and thinly populated, but as the nation grew the majority of voters had no say in who their senators would be. The 17th Amendment rectified (made right) this shortcoming of the Constitution.

Chester A. Arthur, 21st president of the United States. To everyone's surprise, he became a champion of reform and succeeded in getting Congress to create the Civil Service Commission in 1883.

Three other reforms made the American political system more democratic. They are the *initiative*, the *referendum*, and the *recall*. The initiative and the referendum give people some control over lawmaking. The recall allows voters to remove from office elected officials who have failed to carry out their duties.

Through the initiative, voters use a petition to put forth laws they wish to be passed. When enough voters sign the petition, the state legislature must either pass the law or have a special election permitting the people to vote on it. This latter part of the procedure is the referendum. In other referendums, citizens in many states vote on amending state constitutions and other important matters. Thus the referendum provides the people of the various states with a way to check on their legislatures.

The recall also works through a petition. When enough people sign a petition to remove an unpopular or incompetent elected official from office, his or her name is placed on a ballot. The voters then decide whether to keep or remove the official in question.

VOTES

Name _____ Date _____

Take the Initiative

You have learned that the initiative is a way for citizens to have a law put on the ballot for voters to either approve or disapprove. Suppose you and your classmates were able to do the same regarding rules at your school. Which rules would you vote to keep? Which rules would you throw out? Which new rules would you propose?

On the lines provided, respond to the following statements.

1. Two rules at our school that I think are useful and/or necessary are:

   a. _____

   b. _____

   These rules should be continued because _____

   _____

   _____

2. Two rules that I think are unfair or not necessary are:

   a. _____

   b. _____

   These rules, in my opinion, are not good rules because

   _____

   _____

3. In addition to changing or discontinuing the above two rules, I would add three new rules. They are:

   a. _____

   b. _____

   c. _____

   I think these rules would be beneficial because

   _____

   _____

   _____

VOTES

Everyday Life: Reform in America, copyright © Good Year® Books

Name _____ Date _____

Draw Conclusions from What You Have Read

An important part of learning is putting facts together and then arriving at logical conclusions based on what you have read. See how good you are at drawing conclusions from the cases presented.

1. The year is 1880. Bob Trueblue desires to seek his party's nomination as mayor of Colossal City. On the one hand, he is not a member of his party's inner circle, ruled over by corrupt party boss Dillon Villain. On the other, he is honest and feels he has ideas that will help the city.

   What are Bob's chances of getting the nomination? Why?

   _____

2. The year is 1868. Suppose that instead of Ulysses S. Grant becoming president, someone named Thomas Thankworthy is elected instead. President-elect Thankworthy is grateful to those who campaigned hard for him during the election and wants to reward them for their efforts.

   How will President-elect Thankworthy show his gratitude?

   _____

3. The year is 1909. Both the direct primary and the secret ballot have come into use in Colossal City.

   What is likely to happen to Boss Dillon Villain and his party associates?

   _____

4. The year is 1889, six years after the Civil Service Commission was created. Three applicants are competing for a position with the local post office. One applicant has a tenth grade education while the other two have completed two years of college.

   The applicant with the tenth grade education got the job. Why?

   _____

Name _____ Date _____

Distinguish Between Fact and Opinion

Some of the statements on this page are facts; others are only opinions. Put an **F** on the line before each statement you think is a fact, and an **O** before each statement you think is an opinion.

_____ 1. All politicians in the late 1800s were dishonest.

_____ 2. Politicians are justified in giving government jobs to friends and supporters.

_____ 3. Voting by voice vote or by a show of hands deprives people of privacy in making their choices.

_____ 4. The spoils system began during the administration of President Andrew Jackson.

_____ 5. Ulysses S. Grant was the most incompetent of all our presidents.

_____ 6. President Grant was a poor judge of men and character.

_____ 7. Civil service exams make certain that only honest citizens receive government jobs.

_____ 8. The Civil Service Act was passed during the administration of President Chester A. Arthur.

_____ 9. President Grant should have been impeached for the corruption that marked his administration.

_____ 10. The direct primary assures that only the most capable persons become candidates for political office.

_____ 11. Presidential primaries allow voters to participate in the selection of their parties' presidential candidates.

_____ 12. Before the passage of the 17th Amendment allowing for the direct election of U.S. senators, most senators that had been chosen by state legislatures were dishonest and self-seeking.

_____ 13. The initiative gives citizens a voice in the lawmaking process.

Everyday Life: Reform in America, copyright © Good Year Books

Name _____ Date _____

Create a Poster

In the space provided on this page, draw and illustrate a poster demanding the recall of city councilman Dillon Villain, who is also boss of the Moneycratic Party's political machine in Colossal City. List reasons why you think Mr. Villain should be removed from office. Make your poster as colorful and eye-catching as possible.

CHAPTER 10

Conservation

hen European settlers first came to North America more than 400 years ago, they found a land rich in beauty and abundance. Vast forests extended as far as the eye could see, and beyond the forests was a mountain range that stretched from Canada southward to Alabama. Even farther west they found a wide prairie where over 60 million buffalo roamed. Beyond the Great Plains was another mountain range, this one much larger, and beyond it the Pacific Ocean. From east to west, early settlers reaped the benefits of woodlands that teemed with game and lakes, rivers, and streams that literally swam with fish. America was truly a land of plenty.

Buffalo photographed in a range of the Custer State Park of South Dakota. Conservation measures prevented the American bison from becoming extinct.

Even with the Industrial Revolution that followed the Civil War and the settlement of the last frontier (the Great Plains), America was still a beautiful place. Its wonders inspired poet Katharine Lee Bates in 1893 to write the words to the patriotic song "America the Beautiful." The first few lines of her poem paint a picture of America we all know well :

O beautiful for spacious skies, / For amber waves of grain,
For purple mountains majesties / Above the fruited plain!

By the time "America the Beautiful" was written, however, America's beauty and seemingly endless natural resources were in jeopardy. This was because many people thought the land's wealth would last forever, while others simply did not care. Forests were cleared with reckless abandon, and unwise farming methods were practiced. While some settlers followed the soil-preserving methods of farming practiced in Europe, others tilled their land over and over until the ground would no longer produce. They then moved on to unused land, where they cleared more forests and plowed under all

Everyday Life: Reform in America, copyright © Good Year Books

vegetation. The result was that billions of tons of good topsoil were washed yearly into the Gulf of Mexico.

Not only were Americans careless with the land itself, they cared little for conserving the wildlife that inhabited it. As the years passed, many birds and animals were killed to the point of near-extinction. Several did in fact become extinct. Reckless killing wiped out the Carolina parakeet, the Atlantic gray whale, and the passenger pigeon. The latter, once found in large numbers, had all but disappeared by the turn of the 20th century. What was believed to have been the last passenger pigeon in America died in a zoo in 1914.

Another example of an animal driven to near-extinction is the buffalo, or American bison. White hunters in the years following the Civil War almost wiped the animal out. Unlike the American Indian, white hunters were interested only in buffalo hides. They left the carcasses of the animals on the Plains to rot. To add to the slaughter, trains sometimes stopped on the plains and allowed people to shoot buffalo for "sport." By the time most Native Americans had been confined to reservations, the buffalo had almost disappeared from the American scene.

Examples of waste and indifference are endless. During the 1880s some five million birds were killed each year to make fancy hats for women. (An observer in New York City one day counted 20 species of dead birds perched on the heads of women.) One hunter in Louisiana killed 430 ducks in one outing, while another in North Dakota shot 700 pounds of fowl in a period of just four hours! With no laws to restrict them, it is small wonder that irresponsible hunters almost wiped out several species of birds.

Whether it concerned precious land, irreplaceable wildlife, or pollution-free waters, most Americans sat idly by for many years and let waste destroy much of what nature had given them. There were, however, a few naturalists (people who study plants and animals) around who tried to call attention to the problem of conservation. Two in the early years of our country were George Washington and Thomas Jefferson. Both took measures to prevent soil erosion on their estates in Virginia. Two others were Henry David Thoreau and John J. Audubon. Thoreau was a

Henry David Thoreau, noted author and naturalist. He joined others in the struggle to preserve America's wildlife.

Conservationist John Muir stands with President Theodore Roosevelt on a peak above the Yosemite Falls valley of eastern California in 1903. Muir's dedication to conservation had earlier led to the establishment of Yosemite National Park.

naturalist and writer who called for the establishment of areas where wildlife might live in safety. Audubon was an artist whose paintings of birds stirred much interest in their preservation.

One of the earliest conservation measures in the United States was the establishment of Yellowstone National Park in 1872. Located mainly in Wyoming, with parts of it in Idaho and Montana, Yellowstone contains an area of some 3500 square miles. It features, among other things, canyons, lakes, hot springs, and petrified forests. There are also many geysers in the park, the most famous of which is Old Faithful. The park further serves as an animal preserve. Bears, bison, deer, and many different kinds of birds flourish there. Yellowstone Park is not only the largest and oldest national park in the United States; it is also the first to be established worldwide.

Another national park, Yosemite in eastern California, was established in 1890. It became a reality because of the efforts of naturalist John Muir. Yosemite National Park contains almost 1200 square miles. It is noted for its magnificent waterfalls and groves of giant sequoias, or redwood trees. You have probably seen a picture of one tree through which a highway has been cut. It is called the Wawona Tunnel Tree, and thousands of tourists each year drive their automobiles through it. Perhaps you have passed through it yourself.

The person most associated with the birth of conservation in America is President Theodore Roosevelt. In 1901, he began a program of conservation and reclamation. Reclamation refers to making areas such as deserts and swamps suitable for farming. The Reclamation Act of 1902 was aimed at making arid (dry) lands in Nevada, Arizona, and other western states productive. Roosevelt pushed through more than 20 large irrigation projects during his tenure as president. Most of these had to do with the construction of dams. Dams not only provided electricity and irrigation for millions of people but helped to prevent floods as well.

President Roosevelt also urged Congress in 1903 to pass the first Wildlife Refuge Act. This act set aside Pelican Island in Florida as a nesting place for pelicans, herons, and the white ibis. Before he left the White House in 1909,

Everyday Life: Reform in America, copyright © Good Year Books

Roosevelt had helped to establish 51 bird reservations and four big-game refuges in the United States.

The 1906 Antiquities Act provided that regions of scientific and historic value be placed under the protection of the federal government. One such region was Arizona's Petrified Forest. The Antiquities Act saved the stone logs of the forest from gem collectors and souvenir hunters who kept hacking away at them for the amethyst crystals inside. (Amethyst is a form of quartz used in making jewelry.)

A touring family poses after having driven their car through the Wawona Tunnel Tree in Yosemite National Park. The picture was probably taken in the early 1900s.

All told, President Theodore Roosevelt set aside almost 150,000,000 acres of public land as national parks. The number of national parks in the United States doubled during his two terms as President.

President Roosevelt was also responsible for spurring the states to action on conservation. In 1908, he chaired a White House conference of the nation's governors to discuss the preservation of America's resources. Also in attendance were cabinet members, Supreme Court justices, and notable persons in the fields of education, politics, and science. The conference drew national attention to the issue of conservation and led some 27 states to establish conservation commissions of their own.

President Franklin Delano Roosevelt, a distant cousin of Theodore, was another president who championed the cause of conservation. As you will learn in the next chapter, FDR, as he was popularly known, became president during the Great Depression, a bleak time in America's history. To help the economy recover and to provide jobs for the unemployed, FDR started many federal work projects. Some of these projects had to do with conservation, and they formed a part of the president's overall program for helping America recover from the Depression. How FDR helped further the cause of conservation is discussed in the next chapter, entitled "The New Deal."

Name _____ Date _____

Make a Cereal Box Report

In an encyclopedia, almanac, or any book on animals, find and read about an animal in the United States that was or is presently listed as an endangered species (animal on the verge of extinction). After completing your research, prepare a cereal box report for class.

Here are the materials you will need:

1. an empty cereal box, or any similar box

2. white typing or printer paper

3. glue or paste

4. felt-tip pen, or any pen suitable for drawing

5. colored pencils or markers

6. scissors

Here is how to do it:

1. Glue or paste white paper over all sides of the box.

2. On the top edge of the box, write the name of the animal you have researched.

3. On one side panel, write which class your animal belongs to (mammal, bird, reptile, etc.)

4. On the other side panel, write the parts of the United States where your animal is found.

5. On the front of the box, draw and color a picture of your animal.

6. On the back, explain what action the government has taken to protect your animal from extinction.

Be prepared to answer any questions your classmates might have concerning your animal.

Everyday Life: Reform in America, copyright © Good Year Books

Name _____ Date _____

Complete a Word Search

In the word box are 20 nouns from Chapter 10. Find and circle each in the word search. They run horizontally, vertically, and diagonally. None are inverted or backwards.

BUFFALO	**IBIS**	**AMETHYST**
CAROLINA PARAKEET	**AMERICA**	**HERON**
PASSENGER PIGEON	**THOREAU**	**ARIZONA**
NATIVE AMERICANS	**MUIR**	**SEQUOIA**
AUDUBON	**BATES**	**PELICAN**
GREAT PLAINS	**IDAHO**	**YOSEMITE**
NATURALIST	**YELLOWSTONE**	

```
C A R O L I N A P A R A K E E T
A L S T A Y X B A T E S K O S Y
B U F F A L O T S A R S T A T E
I N V E N T O S S T Y C D M F L
N O O G L E G H E J A L M E N L
S A M E R I C A N M R B B T A O
H I G H T E X Y G Z I T H H T W
K T H O R E A U E B Z T E Y U S
B S C D E F G T R H O I E S R T
P E L I C A N S P I N F G T A O
S Q I M P C H D I L A P X Z L N
A U D U B O N K G D A N H H I E
P O L I T E T K E L A I B I S X
L I A R S H E R O N T H N C T M
N A O P Q R S T N U V W O S X Y
N A T I V E A M E R I C A N S Z
```

Name _____ Date _____

Make a List of Conservation Measures

Conservation and protection of our natural resources and environment should be a major concern of all of us. Due to the carelessness and indifference of many, however, the pollution of our air, forests, and waterways pose a serious threat to both our health and our way of life. Unless we shake off our apathy and assume more responsibility for the world in which we live, what we take for granted today may not be here tomorrow.

In the space provided, make a list of any 10 ways you as an individual can help conserve precious resources, as well as keep our environment as clean and as unpolluted as possible.

1. _____
2. _____
3. _____
4. _____
5. _____
6. _____
7. _____
8. _____
9. _____
10. _____

Extension:

Which of the above 10 measures do you consider the most important? Why?

_____
_____
_____
_____
_____
_____
_____
_____

Name _____ Date _____

Make Critical Decisions

Sometimes we are called upon to make critical decisions on important issues or happenings. Such decisions are not easy to make. Our own personal opinion about a specific issue, or our allegiance to friends and acquaintances, often interferes with our ability to do what is right and proper.

Here are two situations having to do with conservation and our environment. Read each carefully and respond to the questions posed.

1. As lumberjacks prepare to cut down trees in a designated forest area, they are confronted by a group of conservationists. These conservationists are concerned about the natural habitat of a rare species of owl. They argue that removing the trees in which the owls nest will bring about their extinction.

   To prevent the loggers from doing their work, several conservationists chain themselves to the trunks of trees. When it becomes apparent that they have no intention of leaving, the boss of the lumberjacks calls for the police to intervene.

   Which group do you think is in the right: the loggers or the conservationists? Why?

   _____

   _____

2. Suppose that because of a severe drought your town is under very tight water restrictions. Residents may water their lawns only once a week, from 8 to 10 on Wednesday mornings. No washing of cars or boats is permitted at any time. Anyone observing a person violating the restrictions is encouraged to call the water police.

   You find yourself in a dilemma. Several times you have seen your neighbor across the street washing his car late at night. You have also noticed his sprinklers going on days other than Wednesday.

   What would you do? Would you call the water police? Why or why not?

   _____

   _____

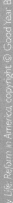

CHAPTER II

The New Deal

Can you imagine a family living in a shack made of tarpaper, cardboard, old signs, and other discarded materials? Can you also imagine such a shack having no stove, running water, windows, or floor? As hard as it is to believe, many people lived in such places during the Great Depression that gripped America from 1929 until the outbreak of World War II.

Shantytowns called "Hoovervilles" (after President Herbert Hoover) sprang up in large cities everywhere. They could be found in city parks, vacant lots, and around garbage dumps. The people who lived in Hoovervilles subsisted on handouts from soup kitchens and from what they could find in dumps and garbage cans. Sometimes children in a family took turns eating; one child might eat on Monday, another on Tuesday, and so on. As hard as these conditions were, they were better than those experienced by homeless people. These unfortunate souls slept under bridges or on sidewalks and park benches. They tried to seek warmth by covering themselves with newspapers. Such "comforters" during the depression years were wryly referred to as "Hoover blankets."

A typical Hooverville. Such shantytowns sprang up across America during the early years of the Great Depression.

The Great Depression began with the stock market crash of 1929. This caused factories and businesses nationwide to close, resulting in millions of Americans being thrown out of work. Those who hoped to survive on their savings were horrified to find their deposits wiped out by the closing of hundreds of banks. Many people avoided starvation by accepting handouts from soup kitchens. Others too proud to accept charity sold apples on street corners, earning a dollar or two a day. During the height of the depression, New York City alone had more than 6,000 apple peddlers.

By 1932, the number of unemployed in America had risen to 12,000,000. (Some sources place the number as high as 14,000,000.)

President Hoover was slow to intervene in the crisis because he believed the depression would be short-lived. He also took the position that hungry and unemployed people should receive aid at the state and local levels. It is not surprising, therefore, that when he ran for re-election in 1932, he suffered a smashing defeat at the hands of the Democratic candidate, Franklin Delano Roosevelt.

A nattily dressed man, obviously once prosperous, sells apples on a street corner in New York City. Many apple vendors made their evening meal from apples that were too bruised or damaged to sell.

Franklin Roosevelt went to work immediately to pull America out of the depths of the depression. On March 9, 1933, five days after his inauguration (presidents were not yet inaugurated on January 20), Roosevelt called Congress into special session. The 99-day period from March 9 to June 16 that followed is referred to as the "Hundred Days." During this time of a little more than three months, the new president proposed more legislation than any president before him had done in his entire term. Because of limited space, however, only some of the reforms carried out during FDR's 12 years in the White House will be covered.

Roosevelt's program for leading the nation to recovery was called the New Deal. The first New Deal measure to go into action was the Civilian Conservation Corps (CCC). It was designed as both a relief and a reform program. In addition to providing work for several million unemployed youth, it served as a way to conserve the nation's vital natural resources. The CCC planted forests and built dams, roads, and recreational facilities. They set up bird sanctuaries, stocked streams with fish, and carried out wildlife surveys. You can witness firsthand much of the work done by the CCC when you visit some of America's state and national parks.

The CCC was organized similar to an army. Young men between the ages of 17 and 33 enlisted and were sent to camps for training. Sometimes they even had to build the camps. There is a story of one recruit who was sent with other enlistees to the wilds of Montana. As he and others dismounted from the trucks that brought them to the site, he inquired of a sergeant as to the whereabouts of the camp. The sergeant replied dryly, "Son, you're standing in the middle of it, and if you don't want to sleep out in the open tonight, you'd best grab an ax and start chopping!"

The CCC saved many young men from poverty and perhaps even lives of crime. Before it disbanded in 1942, some three million recruits went through its rigorous training and on to America's woodlands. They were paid $30 a month and were served three wholesome meals a day. In addition to the financial and health benefits derived from their nine-month enlistments, CCC members gained valuable work experience that served them well later.

Two other New Deal Programs were geared toward construction workers and anyone else who needed a job. The Public Works Administration (PWA) spent more than $4 million on 34,000 public projects. These included the construction of roads and public buildings. For Americans not skilled in construction, the Works Progress Administration (WPA) set up projects to provide them with jobs. In this way, writers, artists, musicians, and actors found gainful employment.

Another of President Roosevelt's programs was the Tennessee Valley Authority, or TVA. The TVA was an agency established in 1933 to develop the natural resources of the region of the Tennessee River and to restore land ravaged by floods. The TVA saw to the construction of dams, power plants, electric transmission lines, and housing projects.

More than 40,000 men found employment with the TVA during the depression years. Besides constructing dams and power plants, they brought erosion under control by planting trees. Because of their labor, new industries were attracted to the Tennessee Valley to take advantage of the cheap electric power and improved navigational facilities afforded by the region.

Franklin Delano Roosevelt, whose New Deal Programs helped end the Great Depression. Immensely popular, FDR stands as the only president to serve more than two terms.

One of the most important reforms urged by President Roosevelt was the Fair Labor Standards Act of 1938, also known as the Wages and Hours Act. You will recall that you were introduced to this act in both Chapters 6 and 8. It established the first minimum wage in America, limited working hours, and brought an end to child labor.

Even before the aforementioned reforms went into effect, President Roosevelt set out to resolve the banking crisis. He did this by allowing only sound banks to operate. He also saw to the establishment of the Federal Deposit Insurance Corporation, which insured depositors' money in the event of a bank

Everyday Life: Reform in America, copyright © Good Year Books

closing. Since that time, people with money in savings or other accounts rest easy knowing that their money is safe and guaranteed by the FDIC.

In carrying out his reforms, President Roosevelt did not forget America's farmers. To help those who tilled the soil, he proposed the Agricultural Adjustment Act. The AAA reduced crop surpluses that had been responsible for falling farm prices. Under the act, the government paid farmers to reduce the amount of land they planted. In the first year after the act went into effect, more than 40 million acres of land were taken out of production. For their cooperation in the effort, farmers were paid several hundred millions of dollars in subsidies (grants of money).

A 1936 photograph of a poor farmer moving his family from one part of Oklahoma to another. Such sights of homeless and displaced persons were common during the depression years.

Many people consider FDR's greatest accomplishment to be the Social Security Act of 1935. This important law initiated a system of old age insurance for workers when they reached the age of 65. It also provided for unemployment payments to people who had lost their jobs. Such a law would have prevented much suffering and poverty had it been in effect when the Great Depression hit in 1929.

Before social security became a reality, elderly people and the unemployed had a difficult time making ends meet. Retirees often had to depend either on their families or on charity to get by. When workers were fired or laid off from jobs, they had no means of income to tide them over until they found employment again. This was the unfortunate fate of many Americans during the years of the Great Depression.

One provision of the Social Security Act guaranteed monthly retirement checks to retired workers over the age of 65. Another provided for survivor's insurance for the children and spouses of insured workers who died. The act also gave federal money to the states to aid needy children, the blind, and other disadvantaged groups.

Today, the Social Security system is in trouble. Experts predict that the system will go broke in the year 2028. When this book went to press, Congress was grappling with a way to insure that future Americans receive the same retirement benefits as do retirees today.

Name _____ Date _____

Brush Up on Your Southern Geography

In Chapter 11 you learned about the Tennessee Valley Authority, or TVA. The Tennessee Valley with which it is associated covers an area of almost 41,000 square miles. Within its borders lie parts of seven southern states: Tennessee, Kentucky, Virginia, North Carolina, Georgia, Alabama, and Mississippi.

How much do you know about the above seven states? Consult an encyclopedia, almanac, or other source to answer the questions on this page.

1. The capitals of the seven states that in part make up the Tennessee Valley are:

State	Capital
Tennessee	_____
Kentucky	_____
Virginia	_____
North Carolina	_____
Georgia	_____
Alabama	_____
Mississippi	_____

2. Which of the above states is the largest in area?
_____

3. Which state has the largest population? (as of 1997)
_____

4. The Great Smoky Mountains, a part of the Appalachian range, lie on the border between the states of _____ and _____.

5. Manassas National Battlefield Park, where the two Battles of Bull Run were fought during the Civil War, is in the state of
_____.

6. Which state is bordered on the east by Georgia and on the west by Mississippi? _____.

7. This state is nicknamed The Bluegrass State.
_____

Everyday Life: Reform in America, copyright © Good Year Books

Name _____ Date _____

Create a Dialogue

Norman and Rocco are two CCC workers at a camp in the Northwest. Norman is grateful to the government for the opportunity to work outdoors, get three nourishing meals a day, and earn a little money. Rocco, on the other hand, has done nothing but complain since the day the camp opened.

Write a dialogue that might have taken place between Norman and Rocco as they discuss life in the CCC.

_____
_____
_____
_____
_____
_____
_____
_____
_____
_____
_____
_____
_____
_____
_____
_____
_____
_____
_____
_____
_____
_____

Name _____ Date _____

Use Context Clues to Complete Sentences

Fill in the blanks using the words from the word box.

accept	completely	plunged
anything	Deal	programs
better	everywhere	street
called	Great	survived
chaos	kitchens	work
closed	names	worst

Presidents like to give their _____ for helping the country special_____.
Woodrow Wilson had his New Freedom, Harry Truman his Fair Deal, and Lyndon Baines
Johnson his Great Society. In Chapter 11, you learned that Franklin Roosevelt _____ his
program the New _____.

The New Deal could not have come at a _____ time for America. The _____
Depression had _____ the nation into economic _____. Banks and factories had
_____, and millions of people were out of _____. Soup _____ and bread
lines became symbolic of cities _____. People too proud to _____ charity
sold apples on _____ corners. Others _____ by rummaging through garbage
dumps for _____ edible. It was truly a sad time in the history of our country.

Although the Great Depression did not _____ end until the beginning of World
War II, the _____ part of it was over by 1934. This was due to the New Deal
programs of Franklin Roosevelt.

Everyday Life: Reform in America, copyright © Good Year Books

Name _____ Date _____

Interpret a Bar Graph

The following graph shows the number of unemployed Americans at various times during the Great Depression. Use the information provided to answer the questions at the bottom of the page.

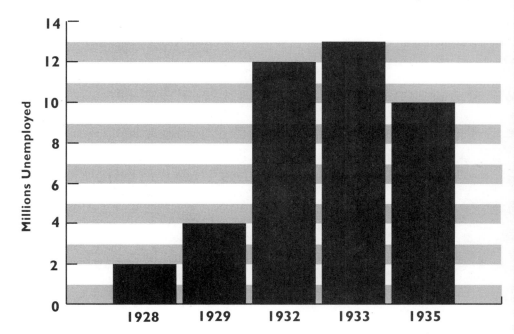

Unemployment During the Great Depression

1. Between which years did the greatest increase in unemployment occur? _____

2. By what percent did unemployment increase between 1928 and 1932? _____%

3. How many less workers were unemployed in 1935 than in 1933? _____

4. By what percent did unemployment decrease between 1932 and 1935? _____%

Civil Rights

Many historians date the beginning of the Civil Rights Movement in America to the *Brown v Board of Education* of Topeka (Kansas) Supreme Court ruling of May 17, 1954. In that historic decision, the U.S. Supreme Court held that the segregation of white and black children in public schools was unconstitutional. The ruling erased the "separate but equal" standard that had been in effect since 1896.

Separate facilities, including water fountains, were the rule in the South until the 1960s.

The "separate but equal" ruling had been no more than a farce. Originally intended to apply to railroad facilities, it was soon twisted to include schools. Schools may have been separate, but they were far from equal. Black schools never had access to the quality of instruction and materials as their white counterparts. As a result, black children were denied the type of education that would guarantee them success in the outside world. Because of such inequity, the Supreme Court issued its famous decision of 1954. More about this—and the family of the little black girl in Kansas who caused it to happen—later.

It could be argued that had the federal government enforced the so-called "Civil War" amendments, there would have been no need for a civil rights movement. In 1865, the 13th Amendment abolished slavery. In 1868, the 14th Amendment granted citizenship to all people born in the United States, which included all freed slaves. And in 1870, the 15th Amendment stated that "no person could be denied the right to vote because of race, color, or previous condition of servitude (slavery)."

So, you might ask, what happened? For starters, once the period of Reconstruction was over in the South, the vengeful North quickly lost interest in the plight of black people. Northerners as a whole had no more thought of granting equal rights to blacks than Southerners. Once slavery had been abolished and the South defeated, they turned their thoughts to other matters.

Temporary gains won by blacks were quickly wiped out when the last federal troops departed the South in 1877. To keep blacks from voting, Southern states passed special laws requiring that would-be voters pay a poll tax and pass a literacy test. Since nearly all blacks were poor, few could pay the tax. Blacks had even more trouble passing the literacy test. Questions centered

Everyday Life: Reform in America, copyright © Good Year Books

around reciting long sections of the state constitution and reading passages written in foreign languages. Even college graduates could not have passed such tests.

Other Southern laws were designed to "keep blacks in their place." They were called "Jim Crow" laws, after the name of a black person in an old minstrel show. Jim Crow laws forbade blacks to use the same facilities as whites. Whether it was a hotel, a restaurant, a library, a park, or a swimming pool, any black who tried to mix with whites was severely punished. Blacks also had to sit in separate sections in theaters, buses, and trains. Bus and railroad stations had restrooms and water coolers labeled "Whites Only."

Prejudice against blacks was not limited to the South. Although Northern states did not pass Jim Crow laws or prevent blacks from voting, they nonetheless discriminated in others ways. They kept blacks from getting good jobs and from buying homes in good neighborhoods. In most Northern cities, blacks were confined to run-down, segregated neighborhoods that came to be called "ghettoes." It was in these areas, as you will learn later in the chapter, that the terrible riots of the 1960s erupted.

Two black leaders with different philosophies emerged in the late 1800s. One was Booker T. Washington, who became famous for founding Tuskegee Institute in Alabama. The other was W. E. B. Du Bois, who, along with others, helped found the National Association for the Advancement of Colored People (NAACP) in 1909. Their proposed ways of helping blacks varied as greatly as their backgrounds.

Booker T. Washington was born a slave on a Virginia plantation in 1856. He was seven years old when the Emancipation Proclamation freed the slaves in 1863. His mother then moved with her children to Malden, West Virginia. There, to help support his mother, brother, and sister, Booker worked in the salt furnaces and coal mines of West Virginia each morning before going to school.

When Booker was 17, he managed to enter Hampton Normal and Agricultural Institute in Virginia. Hampton was a school founded by missionaries for freed slaves. Booker studied hard and graduated in 1875. Afterwards, he taught school for several years before opening Tuskegee Institute in 1881.

Tuskegee Institute was a school designed to teach blacks useful trades. It was Washington's belief that race relations

Booker T. Washington, who founded Tuskegee Institute in 1881. Washington believed that education was the key to black Americans attaining social equality with whites.

with whites would improve if blacks were educated and gainfully employed. He felt that segregation was temporary and that blacks would gain social equality through education.

Not so, maintained W. E. B. Du Bois. Du Bois, who had never been a slave nor known poverty, maintained that blacks should fight for equality in all areas: political and economic, as well as social. To this end, he helped found the NAACP. He later lost patience with the slow progress of the civil rights movement and moved to Africa.

Violence marked the struggle for equality from the late 1800s to the end of World War I. Lynchings in the South and riots in the North were commonplace during these turbulent years. More than 3,000 blacks were lynched in the years between the removal of federal troops in 1877 and the turn of the twentieth century. In the North, race riots stemmed from thousands of blacks moving to the inner cities and competing with whites for jobs.

Although no real progress toward equal rights was made until the 1950s and 1960s, blacks did achieve some milestones in the years between the two world wars. Writer Langston Hughes, tap dancer Bill "Bojangles" Robinson, and actress/singer Ethel Waters began to make their presence known in the late 1920s and 1930s.

Blacks also became superstars in sports. Jesse Owens, a gifted sprinter, won a number of gold medals at the 1936 Olympic Games in Berlin, Germany, much to the chagrin (humiliation) of Nazi dictator Adolf Hitler. Joe Louis won the heavyweight boxing championship in 1937 and held it until 1949. And Jackie Robinson, one of the greatest baseball players who ever lived, became the first black to play in the major leagues when he joined the Brooklyn Dodgers in 1947.

A mother in 1959 explains the significance of the Supreme Court's historic 1954 decision to her young daughter. In that year, the Court ruled that segregation in public schools was unconstitutional.

Five years after Jackie Robinson broke baseball's color barrier, the parents of a seven-year-old girl in Kansas started a lawsuit that in time did the same for the nation's schools. The little girl in question was Linda Brown. When the Topeka, Kansas, school board denied her parents' petition in 1952 that their daughter attend an all-white school, the lawsuit that followed led two years later to the Supreme Court's famous 1954 ruling. Although several years would pass before the ruling was really tested, the case of *Brown v Board of Education* set the civil rights movement into motion.

Everyday Life: Reform in America, copyright © Good Year Books

The following year, an incident in Montgomery, Alabama, added momentum to the young movement. On December 1, 1955, a black seamstress named Rosa Parks refused to give up her seat on a city bus to a white man. Her subsequent arrest started a black bus boycott that lasted 382 days. When it was over, Montgomery's blacks had successfully desegregated that city's buses.

Dr. Martin Luther King, Jr. speaks at a rally during the height of the civil rights movement. King urged black Americans to adhere to a policy of nonviolence in their struggle for equal rights.

From the Montgomery bus boycott emerged a leader who would guide the civil rights movement until his assassination in 1968. That leader was Dr. Martin Luther King, Jr. Dr. King was the pastor of the Dexter Avenue Baptist Church in Montgomery. When the bus boycott began, he urged blacks to counter threats and beatings with nonviolence. Throughout his shortened life, he told blacks that "we must love our white brothers no matter what they do to us."

Dr. King's belief in nonviolence and nonresistance became the guiding principle of the civil rights movement. Throughout the late 1950s and early 1960s, blacks participating in demonstrations, sit-ins, and other activities were taunted, beaten, spit on, and intimidated in other ways. Yet they did not resist. Even when young civil rights workers were murdered in Mississippi, those active in the movement remained passive.

After the Montgomery bus boycott, events moved quickly. In September 1957, Central High School in Little Rock, Arkansas, was integrated, although it took paratroopers from the 101st Airborne Division to do it. In October 1960, sit-ins that began at a lunch counter in Greensboro, North Carolina, quickly spread to 112 other Southern cities. (A sit-in is an organized protest in which demonstrators occupy seats prohibited to them, such as in restaurants or other public places.) And in May of the following year, "freedom rides" began that were designed to desegregate lunch counters and restrooms in bus stations throughout the South. Each of these events resulted in both black and white civil rights demonstrators being severely beaten and jailed. Still, they offered no resistance.

The 1960s were active and violent years in the civil rights movement. In September 1962, James Meredith's desire to attend the University of Mississippi at Oxford, Mississippi, resulted in rioting that took several lives and caused considerable property damage.

But what took place at Oxford paled compared to the violence that erupted in Birmingham, Alabama, in the spring and summer of 1963. In May, Birmingham police used firehoses and dogs to stop demonstrations, one consisting solely of black schoolchildren. What happened in that city in September was even worse. On September 16 a bomb exploded at a church, killing four young black girls.

One month later in Jackson, Mississippi, popular Mississippi NAACP field secretary Medgar Edgars was murdered in the driveway of his home. By this time, President John F. Kennedy had had enough. He submitted to Congress his proposal for a civil rights act—an act that would finally guarantee black people the rights they supposedly had been granted by the 14th and 15th Amendments 100 years earlier.

To show support for the Civil Rights Act, Dr. Martin Luther King staged the famous March on Washington in late August 1963. Some 200,000 people, one-fourth of whom were white, assembled in front of the Lincoln Memorial and heard King's memorable "I Have a Dream" speech. The black leader concluded by saying that, in his dream, he had seen all people holding hands and singing: "Free at last, free at last, thank God Almighty, we are free at last."

The Civil Rights Act that passed Congress in 1964 forbade segregation in public accommodations and public facilities. But because it lacked strong voting rights language, demonstrations throughout the nation continued. In June 1964, three young civil rights workers were brutally murdered in Philadelphia, Mississippi, their bodies savagely beaten and riddled with bullets. In March 1965, thousands of blacks were attacked as they attempted a march from Selma to Montgomery, Alabama, in support of a federal Voting Rights Act. Finally, on April 4, 1968, Dr. King himself was murdered on the balcony of a motel in Memphis, Tennessee. His death caused some 126 riots to break out in cities across America.

In 1965, Congress passed the long-awaited Voting Rights Act. At long last, blacks had achieved, at least on paper, equality with whites. But the struggle for full equality goes on. Prejudice and discrimination still exists against black people everywhere, both in the North and the South. And this book has not even touched on the problems faced by other minorities such as Native Americans, Hispanic Americans, and Asian Americans. Hopefully, some day prejudice and discrimination in America will be a thing of the past.

Name _____ Date _____

Draw Conclusions from What You Have Read

As you read in a similar activity in Chapter 9, an important learning skill is the ability to put facts together and arrive at logical conclusions.

Read each of the statements at the right and write your conclusions on the lines provided.

1. Once slavery was abolished and the South "reconstructed," most Northerners began to occupy themselves with other matters.

   _____

   _____

2. Some blacks in the 1880s referred to Booker T. Washington as an "Uncle Tom."

   _____

3. Instead of the police arresting whites bent on doing harm to freedom riders at bus stations, it was often the freedom riders themselves who were taken to jail.

   _____

4. When President John F. Kennedy was assassinated in Dallas, Texas, on November 22, 1963, most students who heard the news over the intercoms at their schools were shocked. Many wept. However, as the author, who was a young, beginning teacher at the time, remembers, there were a few who applauded and remarked that the president had got what was coming to him.

   _____

   _____

5. In spite of all the achievements made in the field of reform, women who have training and qualifications equal to their male counterparts are often paid less for performing the same job under the same conditions.

   _____

   _____

Name _____ Date _____

Conduct an Interview

Interview someone who remembers well the day Dr. Martin Luther King was assassinated in Memphis, Tennessee, on April 4, 1968. Record where they were at the time, their thoughts upon hearing the tragic news, and the reaction of other people with whom they may have been in contact.

The person you interview can be an older teacher, a family friend, a grandparent, or anyone else who remembers the event. On the lines provided, write a summary of your interview.

Answers to Activities

Chapter 1

Name That Abolitionist
1. Eli Whitney 2. Harriet Tubman 3. Frederick Douglass 4. Henry Brown 5. Samuel Sewall 6. Lucretia Mott 7. Henry David Thoreau 8. Sojourner Truth 9. Levi Coffin 10. Paul Cuffee 11. John C. Calhoun 12. William Lloyd Garrison 13. Benjamin Franklin

Solve Some Antislavery Word Problems
1. 2500 2. 12½ 3. 485,000 4. 2

Use Your Critical Thinking Skills
Students' answers will vary.

Chapter 2

Solve a Women's Rights Crossword
Across: 3. Friedan 4. Lucy 6. Stanton 9. Frederick 12. Anthony 14. Wyoming
Down: 1. London 2. Wilson 5. Suffrage 7. Alice 8. Seneca 10. Lucretia 11. Utah 13. NOW

Distinguish Between Fact and Opinion
1. O 2. O 3. F 4. O 5. F 6. O 7. F 8. O 9. O 10. F 11. O 12. F 13. F 14. O

Chapter 3

Compare Colonial Schools with Modern Schools
Students' answers will vary but should be similar to the following:
1. Type of school building—Colonial Schools: usually a one-room schoolhouse; Modern Schools: large, usually constructed of brick. 2. Heating—Colonial Schools: fireplace; Modern Schools: most have some kind of central heat. 3. Subjects studied — Colonial Schools: religion, 3 "R's;" Modern Schools: well-rounded curriculum. 4. Teacher qualifications—Colonial Schools: no formal training required; Modern Schools: teachers must be certified in education. 5. Discipline—Colonial Schools: often severe; Modern Schools: spankings and other physical punishments are rare today. 6. Length of school year—Colonial Schools: several months; Modern Schools: about nine months. 7. Number of years attended—Colonial Schools: about three years; Modern Schools: twelve years. 8. Attitude toward education for girls—Colonial Schools: girls needed only enough education to make them good wives and mothers; Modern Schools: girls receive the same education as boys.

Use Your Critical-Thinking Skills
Students' answers will vary.

Test Your Knowledge of Massachusetts
1. Atlantic Ocean 2. Vermont and New Hampshire 3. New York 4. Boston 5. eastern 6. cod 7. Plymouth 8. an Indian who befriended and helped the Pilgrims 9. founded the American Red Cross 10. poet 11. inventor

Solve Some Schooling Math Problems
1. 42 2. 6 3. 3 4. 7 5. 8 6. 14 7. 26 8. 10; 5

Chapter 4

Recall Information You Have Read
1. She was Superintendent of Nurses for the Union. 2. They were treated like common criminals, often kept in individual cells that were unheated in winter and stifling in summer. In addition, they were often physically abused. 3. They insisted that prisoners be placed in solitary cells, where they maintained that private meditation would change their behavior and attitude. 4. Congregate and silent system—prisoners were kept in individual cells but allowed to congregate with other prisoners by day, even though they had to remain silent. Separate and silent system—prisoners were kept in individual cells and

had no contact with other prisoners.
5. A special prison for young offenders designed to change their behavior so they can function in the outside world once they are released.

Complete a Prison Questionnaire
Students' responses will vary.

Solve a Dorothea Dix Puzzle
1. Lynde 2. Europe 3. Nurses
   4. fourteen 5. Victoria 6. thirty
   7. teacher 8. Japan 9. debt 10. ill
   11. IX

Name Those Synonyms
Students' answers will vary but might include the following:
1. anger, ire 2. stern, unbending 3. major, principal 4. eliminated, ended
5. measures, criteria 6. change, improve
7. habit, practice 8. kept, restricted
9. uncaring, unconcerned 10. condition, predicament 11. reveal, disclose
12. persuaded, induced 13. requested, entreated 14. isolated, sole
15. changed, altered 16. plan, procedure 17. distinct, particular
18. important, chief 19. free, liberate
20. met, faced

Chapter 5

Use Your Critical-Thinking Skills
1. Cirrhosis (disease of the liver); damage to the heart and stomach; poor nutrition
2. Possible answers include crime, poverty, and family-related problems such as divorce and child or spouse abuse.
3. Answers will vary. 4. Answers will vary.

Distinguish Between Fact and Opinion
1. F 2. O 3. F 4. F 5. O 6. O
   7. O 8. F 9. O 10. F 11. O
   12. F 13. F 14. O 15. O

Interpret a Line Graph
1. 2 2. 24 3. 12 4. That the more one drinks, the longer it takes for the alcohol to leave the body.

Chapter 6

Solve Some Child Labor Math Problems
1. 1200 2. $.04 3. 10 4. 13

Chapter 7

Interpret a Picture
Students' answers will vary but may be similar to the following:
1. She is probably the baby's older sister.
2. To babysit with the baby while her parents are working. 3. Sad, more than likely. 4. Possibly that she wished her life were different than it is. 5. That it is a run-down tenement building.

Complete a Reformer Crossword
Across: 2. Peace 4. doctor 5. Starr
   8. tuberculosis 10. rats 12. London
   13. Chicago 14. tenement 15. Loring
Down: 1. Bureau 3. Addams 6. Hull
   7. Boston 9. Riis 11. Hine
   12. Lowell

Use Context Clues to Complete Sentences
born; father; success; wanted; sympathy; fortunate; accompanying; traveled; shocked; stood; green; children; beside; someday; people; play; years; later

Answer Questions About Tuberculosis
1. consumption; TB; phthisis; white plague
2. a rod-shaped bacteria called tubercle bacillus 3. by repeated exposure to infected persons' coughing and sneezing
4. dry cough and rise in temperature, followed by constant fever; sweating, loss of weight, chest pain, and the coughing up of blood 5. skin tests; x-rays 6. with rest and antibiotics, primarily streptomycin 7. Vaccination with a vaccine called BCG increases the body's resistance to the disease. 8. no

Chapter 8

Tell Why You Agree or Disagree with These Statements
Students' answers will vary.

Solve Some Work-Related Math Problems

1. a. $33.52 b. $23.46 2. $3.50
   3. $92.70 4. $344.25

Indicate Appropriateness of Pay

Students' answers will vary.

Chapter 9

Take the Initiative

Students' answers will vary.

Draw Conclusions from What You Have Read

Students' answers should be similar to the following:

1. Almost nonexistent. Party boss Dillon Villain will decide who the party's candidate will be. 2. He will give government jobs to people who helped him win the election. 3. They will probably be voted out of office. 4. He or she scored the highest on the civil service exam.

Distinguish Between Fact and Opinion

1. O 2. O 3. F 4. F 5. O 6. F 7. O 8. F
   9. O 10. O 11. F 12. O 13. F

Chapter 10

Complete a Word Search

```
C A R O L I N A P A R A K E E T
A L S T A Y X B A T E S K O S Y
B U F F A L O T S A R S T A T E
I N V E N T O S S T Y C D M F L
N O O G L E G H E J A L M E N L
S A M E R I C A N M R B B T A O
H I G H T E X Y G Z I T H H T W
K T H O R E A U E B Z T E Y U S
B S C D E F G T R H O I E S R T
P E L I C A N S P I N F G T A O
S Q I M P C H D I L A P X Z L N
A U D U B O N K G D A N H H I E
P O L I T E T K E L A I B I S X
L I A R S H E R O N T H N C T M
N A O P Q R S T N U V W O S X Y
N A T I V E A M E R I C A N S Z
```

Make a List of Conservation Measures

Students' answers will vary.

Make Critical Decisions

Students' answers will vary.

Chapter 11

Brush Up on Your Southern Geography

1. Nashville; Frankfort; Richmond; Raleigh; Atlanta; Montgomery; Jackson 2. Georgia 3. Georgia 4. Tennessee and North Carolina 5. Virginia 6. Alabama 7. Kentucky

Use Context Clues to Complete Sentences

programs; names; called; Deal; better; Great; plunged; chaos; closed; work; kitchens; everywhere; accept; street; survived; anything; completely; worst

Interpret a Bar Graph

1. 1929 to 1932 2. 600 3. 3,000,000 4. 20

Chapter 12

Draw Conclusions from What You Have Read

Students' answers will vary but should be similar to the following:

1. Northerners lost interest in the plight of blacks and were no more in favor of granting them equal rights than were Southerners. 2. They criticized him for cooperating too much with whites. 3. Police were often on the side of white racists and against civil rights workers. 4. Some Southerners despised President Kennedy because he tried to help America's blacks. 5. Women in America are still looked upon by some men as inferior.

Additional Resources

Books for Children

Freedman, Russell. *Kids at Work: Lewis Hine and the Crusade Against Child Labor.* New York: Clarion Books, 1994.

Hakim, Joy. *A History of US: An Age of Extremes.* New York: Oxford University Press, 1994.

Hazen, Walter A. *The Great Depression.* Grand Rapids, Michigan: Instructional Fair/ TS Denison, 1998.
Women's Suffrage: 1820s–1990s. Grand Rapids, Michigan: Instructional Fair/TS Denison, 1998.

Levin, Nancy Smiler. *Turn of the Century.* New York: Lodestar Books, 1994.

McKissack, Patricia and Fredrick. *The Civil Rights Movement in America: From 1865 to the Present.* Chicago: Childrens Press, 1994.

Books for Adults

Hornsby, Alton Jr. *Chronology of African American History.* Detroit: Gale Research, Inc., 1991.

Sandler, Martin W. *This Was America.* Boston: Little, Brown & Company, 1980.

Weisberger, Bernard A. *The Age of Steel and Steam. Vol. 7, 1877–1890 of The Life History of the United States.* New York: Time Inc., 1964.